SHARE the Music

McGRAW-HILL

AUTHORS

Judy Bond,
Coordinating Author

René Boyer-Alexander

Margaret Campbelle-Holman

Marilyn Copeland Davidson,
Coordinating Author

Robert de Frece

Mary Goetze,
Coordinating Author

Doug Goodkin

Betsy M. Henderson

Michael Jothen

Carol King

Vincent P. Lawrence,
Coordinating Author

Nancy L.T. Miller

Ivy Rawlins

Susan Snyder,
Coordinating Author

Janet McMillion,
Contributing Writer

 **McGraw-Hill School Division**

New York   Farmington

ACKNOWLEDGMENTS

Grateful acknowledgment is given to the following authors, composers, and publishers. Every effort has been made to trace the ownership of all copyrighted material and to secure the necessary permissions to reprint these selections. In the case of some selections for which acknowledgment is not given, extensive research has failed to locate the copyright holders.

Abelard-Schuman for *Chicken on the Fence Post.*

Abilene Music Inc./Gradus Music Co. for *The Eight Days of Hanukkah*. Words and music by George David Weiss.

ACUM Ltd. for *Hag Asif* by Sarah Levy-Tanai and Moshe Rappaport. Copyright © Levy-Tanai & Rappaport Moshe, Israel. English lyrics © Laura Koulish.

Fran Smartt Addicott for *The Delta Queen* by Fran Smartt Addicott. Copyright © Fran Smartt Addicott.

Alfred Publishing Co., Inc. for *Yuki (Snow)* from FAVORITE SONGS OF JAPANESE CHILDREN, translated and collected by Hanako Fukuda. Copyright © MCMLXV by Highland Music Co. Copyright © assigned MCMXC to Alfred Publishing Co., Inc. Used by Permission of the Publisher.

Appalsongs Productions for *The Kindergarten Wall* by John McCutcheon from MAIL MYSELF TO YOU (Rounder 8016). Copyright © 1988 by John McCutcheon/Appalsongs (ASCAP).

Boosey & Hawkes, Inc. for *Gavotta* from SYMPHONIE CLASSIQUE by Sergei Prokofiev. © 1926 by Edition Russe de Musique. Copyright assigned to Boosey & Hawkes Inc., for the world. Reprinted by permission. For *The Piglets' Christmas* (Mary Goetze/Nancy Cooper). Copyright © 1988 by Boosey & Hawkes, Inc. This arrangement is made with the permission of Boosey & Hawkes, Inc. Reprinted by permission.

Butterside Music for *I'll Rise When the Rooster Crows*, lyrics by David Hold. Copyright © 1983 Butterside Music, P.O. Box 8843, Asheville, NC 28814.

W. Jay Cawley for *All Living Things* by W. Jay Cawley. Copyright © 1992 W. Jay Cawley.

Cherry Lane Music Publishing Company, Inc., for *Grandma's Feather Bed* by Jim Connor. Copyright © 1973 Cherry River Music Company. International Copyright Secured. All Rights Reserved.

George M. Cohan Publishing Company for *Yankee Doodle Boy.*

CPP/Belwin, Inc. for *We're Off to See the Wizard* by E.Y. Harburg and Harold Arlen. Copyright © 1938, 1939 (Renewed 1966, 1967) METRO-GOLDWYN MAYER, INC., Rights Assigned to EMI CATALOGUE PARTNERSHIP. All Rights Controlled & Administered by EMI FEIST CATALOGUE, INC. International Copyright Secured. Made in USA. All Rights Reserved.

Curtis Brown Group Ltd. for *They Were My People* from COME INTO MY TROPICAL GARDEN by Grace Nichols. Reproduced with permission of Curtis Brown Group Ltd., London. Copyright © 1988 by Grace Nichols. For *Closet Key* © 1948 by Ruth Crawford Seeger.

Doubleday, Doran & Co. for *Only My Opinion* by Monica Shannon.

Ell-Bern Publishing Company for *Jambo*, words and music by Ella Jenkins, Ell-Bern Publishing Company, ASCAP.

Farrar, Straus & Giroux, Inc. for *Good-bye My Riley O* from SLAVE SONGS OF THE GEORGIA SEA ISLANDS by Lydia Parrish. Copyright © 1942 by Lydia Parrish, copyright renewed © 1969 by Maxfield Parrish, Jr. Reprinted by permission of Farrar, Straus & Giroux, Inc.

Carl Fischer, Inc. for *Waltzing Matilda* adapted by Marie Cowan with lyrics adapted from A.B. "Banjo" Paterson. Copyright © 1936 by Allan & Co. Pty Ltd., Melbourne. Copyright Renewed. Used by Permission. All Rights Reserved.

Frank Music Corp. and Meredith Willson Music for *The Wells Fargo Wagon* by Meredith Willson.

Ganymede Music for *After School* and *Never Gonna Be Your Valentine*, words and music by Linda Worsley. © 1999 by Linda Worsley.

Geordie Music Publishing Co. for *Golden Ring Around the Susan Girl*. © 1963, 1971 Jean Ritchie, Geordie Music Publishing Co. ASCAP. For *Killy Kranky* by Jean Ritchie. Copyright © 1955, 1965 Jean Ritchie, Geordie Music Publishing Co.

Grossett & Dunlap for *Ema Ma* from OUT OF THE EARTH I SING: POETRY AND SONGS OF PRIMITIVE PEOPLES OF THE WORLD. Copyright © 1968 by Richard Lewis. Used by permission of Grosset & Dunlap.

Harcourt Brace Jovanovich, Inc. for *Dance of the Animals* from THE AFRICAN SAGA by Blaise Cendrars, reprinted by permission of Harcourt Brace Jovanovich, Inc.

Harper Collins Publishers, Inc. for *Clink, An Iced Branch Falls* by Kazue Mizumura from FLOWER MOON SNOW: A BOOK OF HAIKU by Kazue Mizumura. Copyright © by Kazue Mizumura. For *Music* from ELEANOR FARJEON'S POEMS FOR CHILDREN by Eleanor Farjeon. Music originally appeared in SING FOR YOUR SUPPER by Eleanor Farjeon. Copyright 1938 by Eleanor Farjeon. Renewed 1966 by Gervase Farjeon. For *Rope Rhyme* by Eloise Greenfield from HONEY, I LOVE by Eloise Greenfield. Text copyright © 1978 by Eloise Greenfield. For *The Secret Song* from NIBBLE NIBBLE by Margaret Wise Brown. Text copyright © 1959 by William R. Scott, Inc. Renewed 1987 by Roberta Brown Rauch.

Patricia Hubbell for *Our Washing Machine.*

Henry Holt and Company for *Mabel, Mabel* from ROCKET IN MY POCKET by Carl Withers. Copyright © 1948 by Carl Withers. Reprinted by permission of Henry Holt and Co., Inc.

Fidelia Jimerson for *Seneca Stomp Dance* by Avery Jimerson. Used by permission.

continued on page 401

McGraw-Hill School Division
A Division of The McGraw-Hill Companies

McGraw-Hill School Division
Two Penn Plaza
New York, NY 10121

Printed in the United States of America
ISBN 0-02-295369-8 / 3
5 6 7 8 9 004 04 03 02 01 00

SPECIAL CONTRIBUTORS

Contributing Writer
Janet McMillion

Consultant Writers
Teri Burdette, Signing
Brian Burnett, Movement
Robert Duke, Assessment
Joan Gregoryk, Vocal Development/
  Choral
Judith Jellison, Special Learners/
  Assessment
Jacque Schrader, Movement
Kathy B. Sorensen, International Phonetic
  Alphabet
Mollie Tower, Listening

Consultants
Lisa DeLorenzo, Critical Thinking
Nancy Ferguson, Jazz/Improvisation
Judith Nayer, Poetry
Marta Sanchez, Dalcroze
Mollie Tower, Reviewer
Robyn Turner, Fine Arts

Multicultural Consultants
Judith Cook Tucker
JaFran Jones
Oscar Muñoz
Marta Sanchez
Edwin J. Schupman, Jr., of ORBIS
  Associates
Mary Shamrock
Kathy B. Sorensen

Multicultural Advisors
Shailaja Akkapeddi (Hindi), Edna Alba
(Ladino), Gregory Amobi (Ibu), Thomas
Appiah (Ga, Twi, Fanti), Deven Asay
(Russian), Vera Auman (Russian, Ukrainian),
David Azman (Hebrew), Lissa Bangeter
(Portuguese), Britt Marie Barnes (Swedish),
Dr. Mark Bell (French), Brad Ahawanrathe
Bonaparte (Mohawk), Chhanda Chakroborti
(Hindi), Ninthalangsonk Chanthasen
(Laotian), Julius Chavez (Navajo), Lin-Rong
Chen (Mandarin), Anna Cheng (Mandarin),
Rushen Chi (Mandarin), T. L. Chi (Mandarin),
Michelle Chingwa (Ottowa), Hoon Choi
(Korean), James Comarell (Greek), Lynn
DePaula (Portuguese), Ketan Dholakia
(Gujarati), Richard O. Effiong (Nigerian),
Nayereh Fallahi (Persian), Angela Fields
(Hopi, Chemehuevi), Gary Fields (Lakota,

Cree), Siri Veslemoy Fluge (Norwegian),
Katalin Forrai (Hungarian), Renee Galagos
(Swedish), Linda Goodman, Judith A. Gray,
Savyasachi Gupta (Marati), Elizabeth Haile
(Shinnecock), Mary Harouny (Persian),
Charlotte Heth (Cherokee), Tim Hunt
(Vietnamese), Marcela Janko (Czech), Raili
Jeffrey (Finnish), Rita Jensen (Danish), Teddy
Kaiahura (Swahili), Gueen Kalaw (Tagalog),
Merehau Kamai (Tahitian), Richard Keeling,
Masanori Kimura (Japanese), Chikahide
Komura (Japanese), Saul Korewa (Hebrew),
Jagadishwar Kota (Tamil), Sokun Koy
(Cambodian), Craig Kurumada (Balkan),
Cindy Trong Le (Vietnamese), Dongchoon Lee
(Korean), Young-Jing Lee (Korean), Nomi Lob
(Hebrew), Sam Loeng (Mandarin, Malay),
Georgia Magpie (Comanche), Mladen Marič
(Croatian), Kuinise Matagi (Samoan), Hiromi
Matsushita (Japanese), Jackie Maynard
(Hawaiian), David McAllester, Mike
Kanathohare McDonald (Mohawk),
Khumbulani Mdlefshe (Zulu), Martin Mkize
(Xhosa), David Montgomery (Turkish), Kazadi
Big Musungayi (Swahili), Professor Akiya
Nakamara (Japanese), Edwin Napia (Maori),
Hang Nguyen (Vietnamese), Richard Nielsen
(Danish), Wil Numkena (Hopi), Eva Ochoa
(Spanish), Drora Oren (Hebrew), Jackie
Osherow (Yiddish), Mavis Oswald (Russian),
Dr. Dil Parkinson (Arabic), Kenny Tahawisoren
Perkins (Mohawk), Alvin Petersen (Sotho),
Phay Phan (Cambodian), Charlie Phim
(Cambodian), Aroha Price (Maori), Marg Puiri
(Samoan), John Rainer (Taos Pueblo, Creek),
Lillian Rainer (Taos Pueblo, Creek, Apache),
Winton Ria (Maori), Arnold Richardson
(Haliwa-Saponi), Thea Roscher (German),
Dr. Wayne Sabey (Japanese), Regine Saintil
(Bamboula Creole), Luci Scherzer (German),
Ken Sekaquaptewa (Hopi), Samouen Seng
(Cambodian), Pei Shin (Mandarin), Dr. Larry
Shumway (Japanese), Gwen Shunatona
(Pawnee, Otoe, Potawatomi), Ernest Siva
(Cahuilla, Serrano [Maringa´]), Ben Snowball
(Inuit), Dr. Michelle Stott (German), Keiko
Tanefuji (Japanese), James Taylor
(Portuguese), Shiu-wai Tong (Mandarin),
Tom Toronto (Lao, Thai), Lynn Tran
(Vietnamese), Gulavadee Vaz (Thai), Chen
Ying Wang (Taiwanese), Masakazu Watabe
(Japanese), Freddy Wheeler (Navajo), Keith
Yackeyonny (Comanche), Liming Yang
(Mandarin), Edgar Zurita (Andean)

CONTENTS

Time for Singing! . . . . **viii**

1 *Theme:*
**GAMES
WE SHARE** **8**

Theme Song:
Swing Up High 10
Greet with a Beat 12
Picture a Melody 18
The Color of Your Voice 24
Playing with Rhythms 28
Playing with Three
    Pitches 34
Alike and Different 38
Musical Choices 42
A Melody Freeze Game 46
REVIEW *Game Songs to*
Remember 50
CHECK IT OUT 52
CREATE/WRITE 53
More Songs to Sing 54

ENCORE
The Orchestra 58

2 *Theme:*
**GOING
PLACES** **62**

Theme Song:
The Happy Wanderer 65
On the Move 66
Designs in Music 70
Traveling by Train 74
    MEET *Steve Reich* 74
Traveling Rhythms 78
Take the Melody Up,
    Up, and Away! 82
Tone Colors of the Moon 86
Sounds of Traveling 90
Picture Your Travels 94
REVIEW *A Return Trip* . . 98
CHECK IT OUT 100
CREATE/WRITE 101
More Songs to Sing 102

ENCORE
Harps Are Everywhere 106
MEET *Alfredo Rolando Ortiz* . . . 108

3 *Theme:* EVERYDAY MUSIC **110**

Theme Song:
Who Will Buy? 112
Everyday Folk Music 114
Song Shapes 118
Conducting Too! 122
Pat Me a Song 126
Two New Pitches in
  the Well 130
Two "Charlies" 134
Road Signs 138
Sing! High, Low, and
  In Between 142
REVIEW *Songs for Every Day* 146
CHECK IT OUT 148
CREATE/WRITE 149
More Songs to Sing 150

ENCORE
Voices from the Heart 154

4 *Theme:* WORDS THAT SING **158**

Theme Song:
Swinging on a Star 160
Simply Silly Story Songs 162
Phrase Your Ideas! 166
Notes that Step, Skip,
  and Repeat 170
Four Sounds to a Beat 174
do—Sing It High, Sing It Low . . . 178
Five Steps to a Melody! 182
Musical Conversations 186
Form Your Ideas 190
REVIEW *Words for the
  Wizard* 194
CHECK IT OUT 196
CREATE/WRITE 197
More Songs to Sing 198

ENCORE
Fit as a Fiddle 202

5 Theme: WORK, PLAY— AND SING 206

Theme Song:
  The Delta Queen 208
Songs for Work and Play 210
An Upbeat Joke! 214
Singing with Added Sounds . . . 218
  MEET *Sally Rogers* 220
Notes that Last 222
Snap It Up! 226
Meter Match 230
Traditions in Song 234
Sharp Contrasts 238
REVIEW *Upbeat Songs* 242
CHECK IT OUT 244
CREATE/WRITE 245
More Songs to Sing 246

ENCORE

  All About the Double Bass 250
    MEET *Milt Hinton* 252

6 Theme: WHAT'S THE NEWS? 254

Theme Song:
  The Wells Fargo Wagon 256
What's the Message? 258
No Bad News! 262
Music with Style 266
  MEET *Midori* 268
Find Your Way Home 272
  MEET *Jean Ritchie* 273
Musical Signs 276
A Message of Good News! 280
Sing Your Message 284
Dance Your Message 288
REVIEW *Songs Making
  the Headlines* 292
CHECK IT OUT 294
CREATE/WRITE 295
More Songs to Sing 296

ENCORE

  The Recording Studio 300

CELEBRATIONS .. 304

From Sea to Shining Sea 306
Trick or Treat 310
Harvest Time 314
Winterfest 318
Eight Days of Light 320
Joy of Christmas 324
Yuletidings 330
From House to House 336
Everybody Says Freedom 338
Be My Valentine 340
Irish Eyes Are Smiling 342
Spring Breezes 344
Voices of the Earth 346
Summer Folk Festival 350

MUSIC LIBRARY 356

MORE SONGS TO READ 356

LISTENING ANTHOLOGY 382
    You're Invited: *Violin Recital* . . . 382
    Listening Discoveries 384

MUSICAL:
Inventive Minds 386

Playing the Recorder 396
Glossary 397
Indexes 403

Time for Singing!

Singing brings people together. When you sing the songs in this unit, you'll be doing the same thing people have done for hundreds of years—singing about what they think and feel, what makes them happy or sad, or even their wishes and dreams.

SING about one person's dream in "I'd Like to Teach the World to Sing."

I'd Like to Teach the World to Sing

Words and Music by Bill Backer, Billy Davis, Roger Cook, and Roger Greenaway

1. I'd like to build___ the world___ a home___
(2.) like to teach___ the world___ to sing___
(3.) like to see___ the world___ for once___

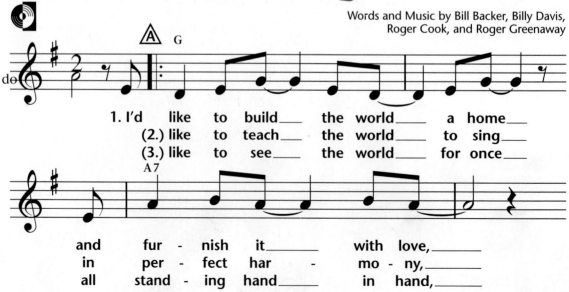

and fur - nish it___ with love,___
in per - fect har - mo - ny,___
all stand - ing hand___ in hand,___

grow ap - ple trees____ and hon - ey bees____ and
I'd like to hold____ it in my arms____ and
and hear them ech - o through the hills____ for

1. C   G
snow white tur - tle - doves.____   2. I'd

2. C   G   3. C   G
keep it com - pa - ny.   3. I'd peace through - out____ the land.

Ⓑ   G   A7
That's the song I hear;____   Let the world sing__ to - day,____

D7   C   G
A song of peace__ that ech - oes on__ and nev - er goes__ a - way.

Time for Singing! **1**

ALPINE SONG

Austrian Yodeling Song
Words Adapted by Susan Van Dyck

1.–4. Oh, an Aus-trian went yo-del-ing on a moun-tain so high.

(1.) When a - long came an a - va-lanche in-ter - rupt-ing his cry.
(2.) When a - long came a Saint Ber-nard in-ter - rupt-ing his cry.
(3.) When a - long came a Guern-sey cow in-ter - rupt-ing his cry.
(4.) When a - long came a Mar - tian in-ter - rupt-ing his cry.

Refrain

Yo - lay - dee, yo - de-lay - hee - hee, Oh yo - de-lay - hee - hoo.

Yo - de - lay - hee - hee, Oh yo - de lay - hee - hoo.

Yo - de - lay - hee - hee, Oh yo - de - lay - hee - hoo.

Yo - de - lay - hee - hoo - oh lay.

Insert on each verse as follows:

1. shh-shh . . .

2. pant-pant, shh-shh . . .

3. moo-moo, pant-pant, shh-shh . . .

4. beep-beep, moo-moo, pant-pant, shh-shh . . .

Cowboys of the western plains sang many
songs such as this one while they worked.

Home on the Range

American Cowboy Song

1. O give me a home where the buf-fa-lo roam, Where the
2. The air is so pure and the zeph-yrs so free, And the
3. How of-ten at night when the heav-ens are bright, With the

deer and the an-te-lope play,— Where sel-dom is heard a dis-
breez-es so balm-y and light,— That I would not ex-change my—
light from the glit-ter-ing stars,— Have I stood there a-mazed and—

cour-ag-ing word, And the skies are not cloud-y all day.—
home on the range For— all of the cit-ies so bright.—
asked as I gazed, If their glo-ry ex-ceeds that of ours.—

Refrain

Home, home on the range,— where the deer and the an-te-lope

play,— Where sel-dom is heard a dis-cour-ag-ing word, And the

skies are not cloud-y all day.—

"Rockin' Robin" was a 1950s rock 'n' roll hit. The beat and rhythm make people want to move.

Rockin' Robin

Words and Music by
Jimmie Thomas (Leon René)

Swing

C   3   3   F   3   G7   3   *Repeat 3 times*

Twee- dl- ee dee-dl- ee dee,   twee- dl- ee dee-dl- ee dee,

C

tweet,   tweet,   tweet tweet!   1. He

Verse
C7   3

1.,3. rocks in the tree- top all_____ the day long,___ hop-
2. Ev-'ry lit-tle swal-low, ev - 'ry chick-a- dee,___ ev -

C7

- pin' and a bop- pin' and a sing- in' his song. All___
- 'ry lit-tle bird_____ in the tall___ oak tree. The

C7   3

___ the lit- tle birds on___ Jay- bird street,___ love___
wise___ old owl and the big black crow,___ flap -

C7

___ to hear the rob- in go- in' "Tweet, tweet, tweet!"⎫ Rock- in'
- pin' their___ wings___ sing- in' "Go, bird, go!" ⎭

Refrain
F7   C7

Rob- in,   Rock- in' Rob- in,

African Americans have created many songs that Americans love to sing. Like other songs in this book, "Michael, Row the Boat Ashore" has been passed along from parent to child and from friend to friend. Now it will be your turn to pass it along.

African American Spiritual

Call — D — *Response* — G — D

1. Mi - chael, row the boat a - shore, } Hal - le - lu - jah!
2. Sis - ter, help to trim the sails, } Hal - le - lu - jah!

Call — F#m — Em — *Response* — A7 — D

Mi - chael row the boat a - shore, } Hal - le - lu - jah!
Sis - ter, help to trim the sails, } Hal - le - lu - jah!

3. River Jordan is deep and cold, . . .
   Chills the body but not the soul, . . .

4. Michael's boat's a music boat, . . .

5. Michael, row the boat a-shore, . . .

George M. Cohan is known for his spirited songs, plays, and musicals. The energetic march on the next page celebrates our flag.

You're a Grand Old Flag

Words and Music
by George M. Cohan

You're a grand old flag, you're a high-fly - ing flag;

And for - ev - er in peace may you wave; _____

You're the em - blem of the land I love,

The home of the free and the brave. _____

Ev' - ry heart beats true un - der red, white, and blue,

Where there's nev - er a boast or brag; _____

But should auld ac - quaint - ance be for - got,

Keep your eye on the grand old flag. _____

GAMES WE SHARE

Rope Rhyme

Get set, ready now, jump right in
Bounce and kick and giggle and spin
Listen to the rope when it hits the ground
Listen to the clappedy-slappedy sound
Jump right up when it tells you to
Come back down, whatever you do
Count to a hundred, count by ten
Start to count all over again
That's what jumping is all about
Get set, ready now
jump
right
out!

—Eloise Greenfield

9

The games we play use rhythm in much the same way that music does. When you swing, your body moves in a rhythmic motion to send your swing higher. Sometimes you hear the swing creak in rhythm as you sail up and back. Hear and feel the rhythm of swinging as you sing this song.

Swing Up High

Words and Music by Joe Raposo

1.–3. Swing up high,_____ swing up free,_____

(1.) no - bod - y's gon - na swing as high as me._____
(2.) look a - round and see the pret - ty things I see._____
(3.) think a - bout the high - est thing that you can be._____

Swing up high,_____ swing up free,_____

come and swing a - long with me._____

10

B D

D7　　　　G

Sun - shine morn - in' break- ing　o - ver - head;———

C　　　　　　　　　　　　　　　　　　Em

come on, la - zy - bones, get　out——　of bed.———

C　　　　　　　　　　　A7

Takes a lot of work to get to touch the sky,——　and you're

Go back to the beginning and sing to the end

(D.C. al Fine)

D　　　　　　　G　　　　D7

real - ly gon - na have to try.———

GREET With a

How do you greet your friends? If you went to Africa, you might say *Jambo*. If you lived in Japan, you'd say *Konichiwa*. Spanish-speaking people say *Hola*.

SING "Jambo" as you wave hello to a friend.

Jambo
▪ Hello ▪

Words and Music
by Ella Jenkins

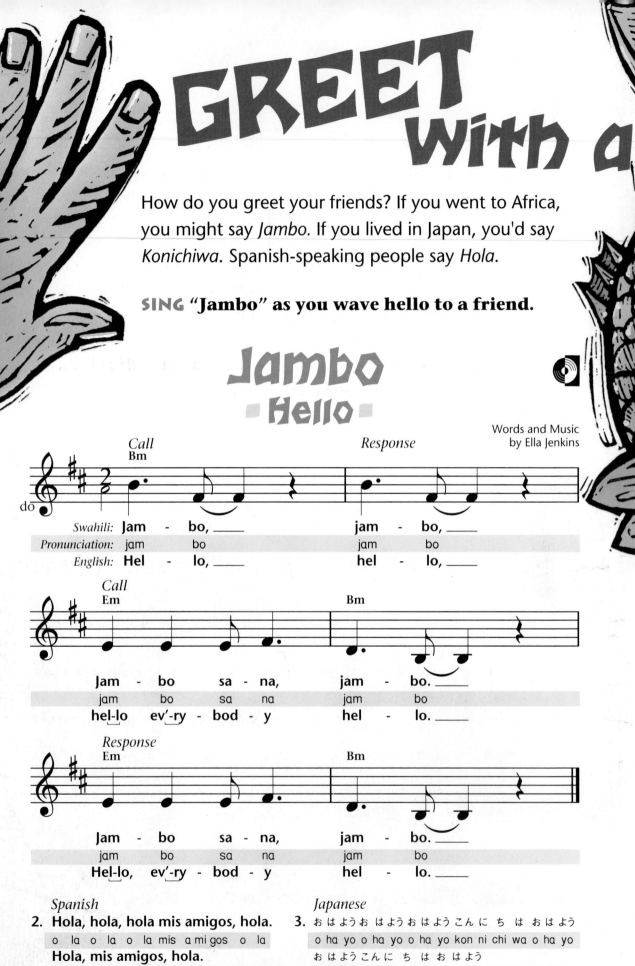

Call
Bm

Swahili:	**Jam** -	**bo,** _____	jam -	bo, _____
Pronunciation:	jam	bo	jam	bo
English:	**Hel** -	**lo,** _____	hel -	lo, _____

Call
Em / Bm

Jam - bo sa - na, jam - bo. _____
jam bo sa na jam bo
hel-lo ev'-ry - bod - y hel - lo. _____

Response
Em / Bm

Jam - bo sa - na, jam - bo. _____
jam bo sa na jam bo
Hel-lo, ev'-ry - bod - y hel - lo. _____

Spanish
2. **Hola, hola, hola mis amigos, hola.**
o la o la o la mis a mi gos o la
Hola, mis amigos, hola.
o la mis a mi gos o la

Japanese
3. おはようお はようお はようこんに ち は おはよう
o ha yo o ha yo o ha yo kon ni chi wa o ha yo
おはようこんに ち は おはよう
o ha yo kon ni chi wa o ha yo

12

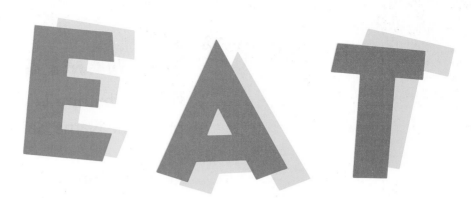

BEAT

Children in Cleveland, Ohio, made up this funny rhyme. They used the **rhythm of the words** to make the rhyme into a **speech piece.**

LISTEN to the speech piece "Bonefish, Bluebird" and tap each bar with the *steady beat.*

Speech piece by Ruth Hamm and
Isabel McNeill Carley
Words Adapted by MMH

Bone-	fish,	blue-	bird,	sheep	and	flea,
Chick-a-	dee,	doo-dle	bug,	rob-ins	in a	tree.
Fly	in the	cream	jar.	Frog	in the	pool.
Clap for all	the	chil-	dren	here	at	school.

FIND the beat of silence in each line.

COMPARE the beat with the rhythm of the words. How are they different?

THE NAME GAME

Use the rhythms in your names to play "The Name Game."

SAY the name of a classmate on Beats 1 and 2 as you tap your right fist on your left fist. Say nothing on Beats 3 and 4 as you tap your left fist on your right fist.

Beat 1	Beat 2	Beat 3	Beat 4

Beats with sound   Beats with silence

PLAYING WITH PATTERNS

Children in Ghana, a country in Africa, use rhythms to play a stone-passing game. You can learn the rhythms and the game, too!

PAT on Beats 1 and 2. Make no sound on Beats 3 and 4.

Which beats have sound? Which beats have silence? This four-beat pattern is called a **rhythm pattern** because it repeats.

Pat left
Beat 1

Pat right
Beat 2

Thumbs
Beat 3

Thumbs
Beat 4

You can use the four-beat rhythm pattern with "Ɔboɔ Asi Me Nsa," a song from Africa. The pattern will help you to play the stone-passing game.

LISTEN to "Ɔboɔ Asi Me Nsa" as you pat the four-beat rhythm pattern.

Ɔboɔ Asi Me Nsa

Akan Stone-Passing Game

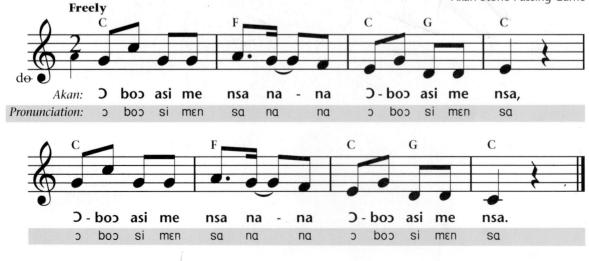

Akan: Ɔ boɔ asi me nsa na - na Ɔ-boɔ asi me nsa,
Pronunciation: ɔ boɔ si mɛn sa na na ɔ boɔ si mɛn sa

Ɔ-boɔ asi me nsa na - na Ɔ-boɔ asi me nsa.
ɔ boɔ si mɛn sa na na ɔ boɔ si mɛn sa

THINK IT THROUGH

What music games do you enjoy? How are rhythms and music used in games and sports?

Next time you're playing a game, choose words and rhythms to create your own speech piece. Then say your speech piece as you play.

"BANANA KELLY" DOUBLE DUTCH

The American artist John Ahearn created this sculpture in 1982. It is located on the apartment building where the four girls live. The building is in the Bronx, New York.

A mountain range has high peaks and low valleys. When you sing, your voice makes high and low sounds, or **pitches**. A line of pitches that moves up, down, or repeats is called a **melody**.

LISTEN to "Rocky Mountain" as you trace the shape of the melody below.

Appalachian Folk Song

ROCKY MOUNTAIN

tain high,

moun-

tain,

tain,

Rock-y moun-

rock-y moun-

rock-y

A Melody

When you're on that rock-y moun-tain,

hang your head and cry.

Refrain:
Do, do, do, do, Do remember me.
Do, do, do, do, Do remember me.

2. Sunny valley, sunny valley,
   sunny valley, low,
   When you're in that sunny
   valley, sing it soft and slow.
   Refrain

3. Stormy ocean, stormy ocean,
   stormy ocean wide,
   When you're in that deep
   blue sea, there's no place
   you can hide.
   Refrain

DANCE A STORY

Songs like "Rocky Mountain" tell stories with words and music. A **ballet** tells a story using dance and music.

LISTENING

by Aram Khachaturian

The ballet Gayane *tells about men who try to steal from some farmers.*

The farmers find out about the robbers and catch them. Because the farmers are happy, they dance the "Sabre Dance."

TRACE the shape of the "Sabre Dance" melody. Does the melody move mainly up, down, or with repeated pitches?

INTRODUCTION
16 beats

Ⓐ MAIN THEME

a   a

a'   a'

Ⓑ 𝄆

① ②

flute second time

③ ④

𝄇

BRIDGE

▵A'

a   a'

a'

CODA

Here's a chance for you to find "peaks" and "valleys" in another melody.

LISTEN to "Long-Legged Sailor" and trace the shape of the melody.

Did you ev- er, ev- er, ev- er in your long- leg- ged life

Meet a long- leg- ged sail- or with a long- leg- ged wife?

FIND words in a row that repeat.

Does the melody move up, down, or repeat on those words?

THINK IT THROUGH

Compare the shape of this melody with the "Sabre Dance" theme. How are they alike?

The Color of Your Voice

You have your very own fingerprint.

You also have your own voice print. A voice print of your singing might look like this.

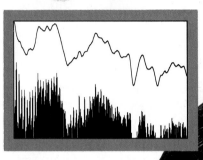

A voice print of a friend's singing might look like this.

The special sound of your voice is called its **tone color**.

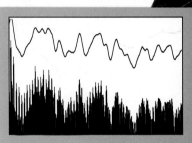

SAME VOICE, DIFFERENT TONE COLORS

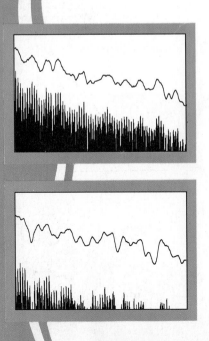

You can make heavier and lighter sounds with your voice. This picture shows a person singing a pitch in a **heavier voice**.

This picture shows the same person singing the same pitch in a **lighter voice**.

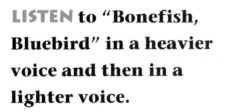

LISTEN to "Bonefish, Bluebird" in a heavier voice and then in a lighter voice.

CHOOSE your heavier or lighter voice and say "Bonefish, Bluebird."

THINK IT THROUGH

How does saying "Bonefish, Bluebird" in a heavier or lighter voice change its feeling?

SINGING WITH TWO VOICES

Just as you can speak in a heavier or lighter voice, you can sing in a heavier or lighter voice. Listen to "Down by the River" sung both ways.

CHOOSE your heavier or lighter voice to sing this song.

African American Singing Game

1. Down by the river two by two, two by two, two by two.
   Down by the river two by two, now rise Sally rise.

2. Let me see you make a motion two by two, . . .

3. Now take another partner two by two, . . .

INSTRUMENTS HAVE TONE COLORS, TOO!

Each musical instrument, like each voice, has its own special tone color.

LISTEN for the tone colors of these instruments and play a game.

When you hear the triangle, stand and slowly move your arms.

Shake and jiggle when you hear the tambourine.

When you hear the woodblock, walk with a quick step.

PLAYING WITH RHYTHMS

AFRICA

Ghana

Children in Ghana, Africa, perform movements as they play stone-passing games. You can enjoy one of these games with the song "Ɔboɔ Asi Me Nsa." Sit in a circle and say *grab, pass, thumbs, thumbs* as you listen to "Ɔboɔ Asi Me Nsa."

SING "Ɔboɔ Asi Me Nsa" as you play the stone-passing game.

Grab

Pass

Thumbs

Thumbs

29

ROCKY MOUNTAIN RHYTHMS

The rhythm of "Rocky Mountain" has one sound,
two sounds, and no sound to a beat.

quarter note (one sound)   eighth notes (two sounds)   quarter rest (no sound)

**CLAP the rhythm of "Rocky Mountain"
as you say the words.**

Rock - y   moun-tain, rock - y   moun-tain, rock - y   moun-tain   high,

The **meter signature** ² of "Rocky Mountain"
tells you that the beats are felt in sets of two. Each set
of two beats is called a **measure. Bar lines** separate
the measures.

CLAP this rhythm as you say *rock* for ♩ and *moun-tain* for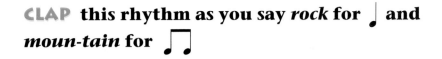

How many measures are in this rhythm?

"Rocky Mountain" was first sung by people who lived near the Appalachian Mountains. This area is a center for the folk arts, such as making dolls, baskets, quilts, and dulcimers.

A "SURPRISING" RHYTHM!

The rhythms in "Rocky Mountain" can be found in much of the music you sing, play, or listen to.

READ these rhythms, saying *tip-toe* for ♫ and *look* for ♩

1. [music notation]

2. [music notation]

"Surprise" Symphony
LISTENING

No. 94, Second Movement (excerpt)
by Franz Joseph Haydn

LISTENING MAP *Tap on the pictures in this listening map as you listen to the "Surprise" Symphony.*

MOVE as you listen to the "Surprise" Symphony again. Say the words *tip-toe* and *look* as you move. On the last note say *jump*, and make the largest shape you can.

Which of these rhythms is repeated in the first part of the "Surprise" Symphony? Which of these rhythms has the "Surprise" in it?

1.

2.

Spotlight on Franz Joseph Haydn

Franz Joseph Haydn (1732–1809) was an Austrian composer who wrote the "Surprise" Symphony for a special after-dinner concert. He knew that many of the people might be using this concert as their nap time, so he used calm string music. He gave them just enough time to doze and then CRASH! The whole orchestra played a chord as loud as possible.

PLAYING

The game song "Kuma San" uses three pitches. Children in Japan sing "Kuma San" as they jump rope. The words tell you how to move.

TRACE the shape of the melody on the words Kuma San.

KUMA SAN
Honorable Bear

Japanese Folk Song
English Version by
Marilyn Davidson and
Kathy B. Sorensen

Japanese: く ま さん く ま さん まわれ み ぎ
Pronunciation: ku ma san ku ma san ma wa ɾe mi gi
English: Ku - ma san, ku - ma san, turn your-self a - round.

く ま さん く ま さん りょう て を つい て
ku ma san ku ma san ɾyo te wo tsui te
Ku - ma san, ku - ma san, hands up - on the ground.

く ま さん く ま さん か た あ し あげ て
ku ma san ku ma san ka ta a shi a ge te
Ku - ma san, ku - ma san, jump with one foot in the air.

く ま さん く ま さん さ よ う な ら
ku ma san ku ma san sa yo u na ɾa
Ku - ma san, ku - ma san, Sa - yo - u - na - ra.

WITH THREE PITCHES

SING "Kuma San" and touch your legs on the lowest pitch, your waist on the middle pitch, and your shoulders on the highest pitch.

Mi is the highest pitch.

Re is the middle pitch.

Do is the lowest pitch.

Pitches are written on a **staff** that has five lines and four spaces. The lines on a staff are numbered from the bottom up. What number is the top space? Top line?

Spaces

Lines

This staff shows the three pitches used in "Kuma San." In which space is *do*? *mi*? On which line is *re*?

do   *re*   *mi*

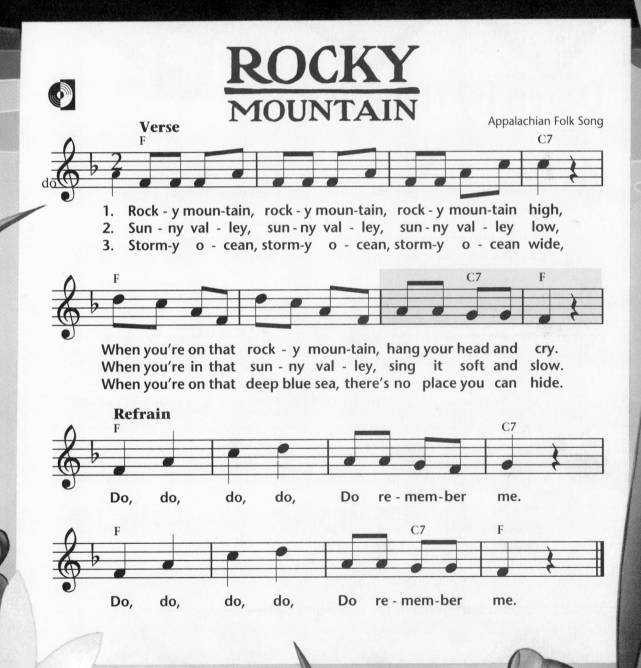

You can see alike and different everywhere: on your clothes, in the playground, and even in this song.

ALIKE AND

Down by the River

African American Singing Game

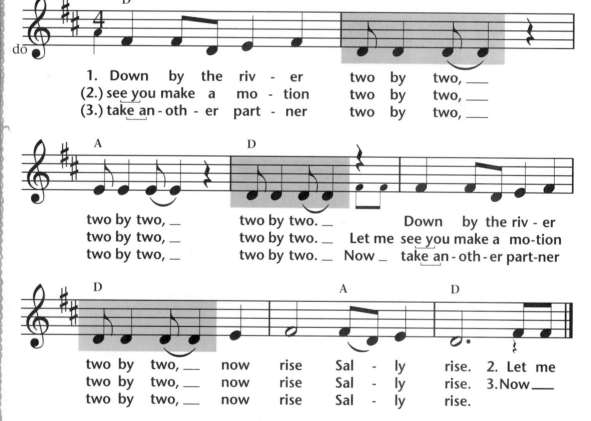

1. Down by the riv - er   two by two, ___
(2.) see you make a mo - tion   two by two, ___
(3.) take an - oth - er part - ner   two by two, ___

two by two, _   two by two. _   Down   by the riv - er
two by two, _   two by two. _   Let me see you make a mo-tion
two by two, _   two by two. _   Now _ take an - oth - er part-ner

two by two, ___   now   rise   Sal - ly   rise. 2. Let me
two by two, ___   now   rise   Sal - ly   rise. 3.Now___
two by two, ___   now   rise   Sal - ly   rise.

Which measures in "Down by the River" are alike?

DIFFERENT

FINDING "DO" IN A DIFFERENT PLACE

Where is *do* in the song "Kuma San"?

Here is *do* in a different place—beneath
Line 1. *Re* and *mi* are always just above *do*.

SING **"Down by the River" using
pitch syllable names.**

The cook in this song is looking for what item?

DUMPLIN'S

West Indian Calypso Song
New Words and New Music Adaptation by
Massie Patterson and Sammy Heyward

"Cook-ie, _____ did you see a'-bod-y pass here?"

"No, my friend." "Cook-ie, _____ are you sure no-bod-y passed here?"

Refrain
Faster, with rhythm

"No, my friend." "Well {one two} of my dump-lin's

gone." "Don't tell ___ me so!" {"One "Two} of my dump-lin's

gone." "Don't tell __ me so!" {"One "Two} of my dump-lin's gone!"

FIND the parts of "Dumplin's" that are alike.

Now find *do* in "Dumplin's."
Then sing the pattern *No, my friend* using
pitch syllable names.

SIXTEEN HENS

The artist, Blanchard, is from the island of Haiti,
part of the Caribbean Islands, where people first
sang "Dumplin's." Blanchard used many shapes
that are alike in this painting. Can you find
three shapes that are alike? Three shapes
that are different?

MUSICAL Choices

Haydn made many musical choices when he composed the "Surprise" Symphony. He chose:

rhythms

sounds and silences

pitches

higher and lower sounds

tone colors

the special sound of instruments and voices

You can make some choices about music, too! Start with the rhythm. Choose where the silence comes in the rhythm.

CLAP these rhythms. Then move to them. Move on the beats with sound. Rest on the beats with silence.

Which beat has no sound? What is the symbol for no sound on a beat?

CREATE your own rhythm patterns. Choose where to put the rest.

DYNAMICS: SOFT AND LOUD IN MUSIC

You can also make choices about **dynamics** in music. Dynamics are the softness or loudness of musical sounds.

LISTEN for soft and loud notes in the "Surprise" Symphony.

In music, *p* means *piano*. It means to sing or play the music *soft*. An *f* means *forte*. It means to sing or play the music *loud*.

What might *pp* mean?
What might *ff* mean?

SING this part of "Dumplin's" with these dynamics.

p   *f*
Well one of my dumplin's gone. Don't tell me so!

p   *f*
One of my dumplin's gone. Don't tell me so!

p
One of my dumplin's gone!

NOW sing "Dumplin's" with these dynamics.

f   *p*
Well one of my dumplin's gone. Don't tell me so!

f   *p*
One of my dumplin's gone. Don't tell me so!

f
One of my dumplin's gone!

THINK IT THROUGH

Sing "Dumplin's" with the dynamics you choose. Compare the ways you sang "Dumplin's." Which way do you like better? Why?

A MELODY FREEZE GAME

In this game you can move to the three pitches you know.

LISTEN to "Melody Freeze." Do you hear the last pitch of each phrase "freeze"? Freeze to show which pitch you hear.

MELODY FREEZE

mi re do   mi re do   mi mi   ?

mi re do   mi re do   re re   ?

mi re do   mi re do   mi mi   ?

mi re do re   mi mi mi mi   mi re   ?

do   re   mi

A **fermata** (⌒) placed over a note shows where the melody freezes. It tells you to hold the note longer than usual.

SING this melody with fermatas and guess the song.

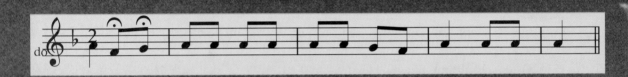

The Hungry Waves

The hungry waves along the shore
Chase each other with a roar.

They raise their heads and, wide and high,
Toss their hair against the sky.

They show their teeth in rows of white
And open up their jaws to bite.

—Dorothy Aldis

THINK IT THROUGH

Which words of this poem might you
hold? Why did you choose these words?

GAME SONGS TO REMEMBER

You've learned some games that children in different countries play. What songs do these pictures remind you of?

Create a news program about the game songs. Choose someone to be the interviewer. Then form groups of three or four, and play one of the games. When the interviewer comes to your group, sing the song and show how the game is played.

CHECK IT OUT

1. You will hear a song with a drum playing along. What is the drum playing?

   a. the rhythm

   b. the beat

   c. changes from rhythm to beat

2. You will hear a song with a drum playing along. What is the drum playing?

   a. the rhythm

   b. the beat

   c. changes from rhythm to beat

3. How does this melody move?

   a. upward ↗

   b. downward ↘

   c. repeats on the same pitch →

   d. upward then downward ↗ ↘

4. Which rhythm do you hear?

5. What pitches do you hear?

52

CREATE

Make Your Own Rhythm Pattern

Draw eight boxes on a piece of paper.

- Put 2 eighth notes (♪♪) in 2 or 3 boxes.
- Put a quarter note (♩) in 2 or 3 different boxes.
- Put a quarter rest (𝄽) in the other boxes.

CREATE a melody for your rhythm using the bells *do* (F), *re* (G), and *mi* (A).

F   G   A

Add a surprise to your melody by playing a part of it loud.

Write

Think about the game songs that you like most. Write a letter to a child who lives in the country from which your favorite game comes.

- Describe what you enjoy about the game.
- Tell about a game that you play.

Oma Rapeti
Run, Rabbit

New Zealand Folk Song
Collected and Transcribed by Kathy B. Sorensen

Maori: O-ma ra - pe-ti, o-ma ra - pe-ti, o-ma __ o-ma o-ma! __
Pronunciation: o ma ɾa pɛ ti o ma ɾa pɛ ti o ma o ma o ma

Kau - a ri - ro kau-a ri - ro koe ai - a. _____
ko a ɾi ɾo ko a ɾi ɾo koe aɪ a

Ka o - ra i - he-i a-ha ra - pe - ti. _____
kɑ o ɾa i he ɪ a ha ɾa pɛ ti

O-ma ra - pe-ti, o-ma ra - pe-ti, o-ma __ o-ma o-ma! __
o ma ɾa pɛ ti o ma ɾa pɛ ti o ma o ma o ma

English: Run, rab - bit, run, rab - bit, run, run, run!

Don't give _ the far - mer _ his fun, fun, fun.

He'll get by with - out his rab-bit ___ pie,

so run, rab - bit, run, rab - bit, run, run, run!

Miss Mary Mack

African American Singing Game

1. Miss   Ma - ry   Mack,   Mack,   Mack,
2. She   asked her moth-er,   moth-er,   moth-er,
3. They   jumped so high,   high,   high,

All   dressed in   black,   black,   black,
For   fif - ty   cents,   cents,   cents,
They   reached the   sky,   sky,   sky,

With   sil - ver   but-tons,   but-tons,   but-tons,
To   see the   cows, __   cows, __   cows, __
And   nev-er came   back, __   back, __   back, __

All   down her   back,   back,   back.
Jump   o-ver the   fence,   fence,   fence.
Till the Fourth of Ju - ly,   lie,   lie!

After School

Words and Music
by Linda Worsley

1. Do you want to come o - ver to my house? __
(2.) bor-row a ball __ and shoot bas - kets? __
(3.) have to be home __ be - fore sup - per, __

Do you want to come o - ver and play?
Can we play with some vi - de - o games?
And I have to be home __ be - fore dark,

There's a tree we can climb, __ and plen-ty of time __ af - ter
There's a puz-zle to make, __ We'll eat ap-ples and cake __ af - ter
It's a time we can play, __ the best time of the day __ af - ter

1.
school. 2. Can I school. 3. Well, I

3.
school. Come o - ver af - ter school, Come on! __

Come o - ver af - ter school! O K!

encore the Orchestra

Look at the pictures of the instruments. What kinds of sounds do you think they make when they are played?

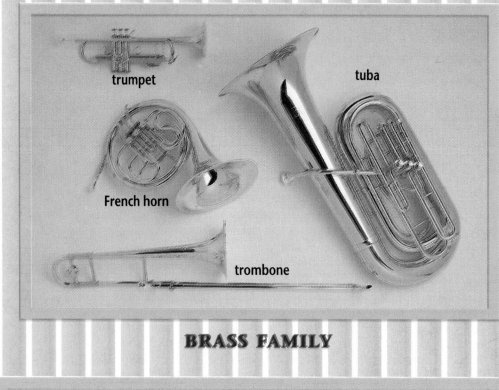

BRASS FAMILY

trumpet

tuba

French horn

trombone

double bass

harp

cello

violin   viola

STRING FAMILY

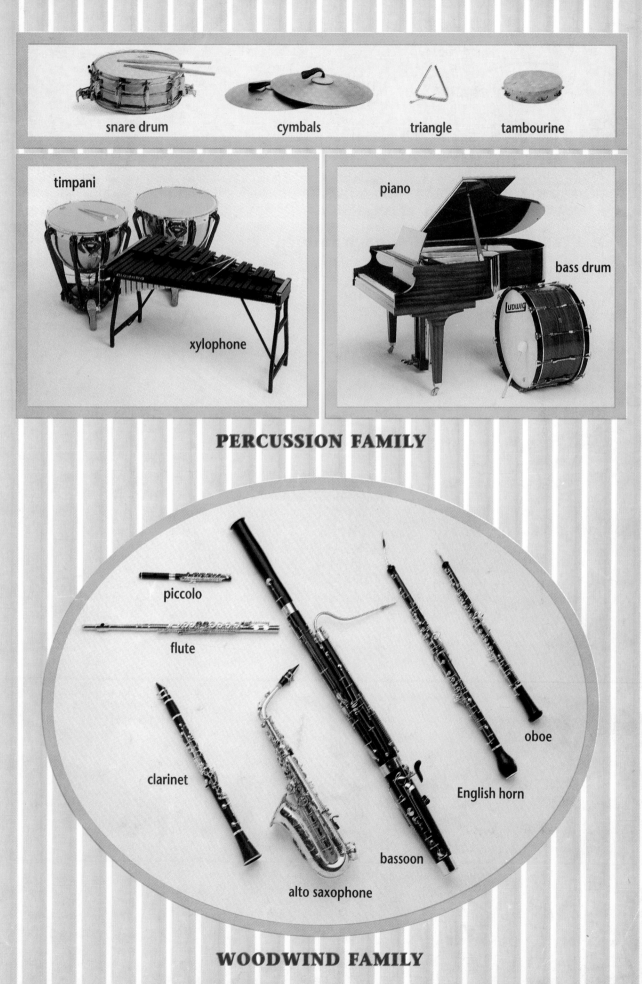

snare drum

cymbals

triangle

tambourine

timpani

xylophone

piano

bass drum

PERCUSSION FAMILY

piccolo

flute

clarinet

alto saxophone

bassoon

English horn

oboe

WOODWIND FAMILY

LISTENING

Montage of Orchestral Sounds

The orchestra has four families of instruments.

LISTEN for the sound of each family.

1. Woodwind family
2. String family
3. Percussion family
4. Brass family

Variations on the Theme *Pop! Goes the Weasel*
by Lucien Caillet

Lucien Caillet used an American folk song in his music for orchestra.

SING the song, then listen for the four instrument families in Caillet's music.

POP! GOES THE WEASEL

American Ring Game

do

| F | C7 | F | | C7 | F |

All a-round the cob - bler's bench, The mon-key chased the wea-sel.

| F | C7 | F | B♭ | C7 | F |

The mon-key said 'twas all __ in fun. Pop! goes the wea - sel.

BICYCLE RIDING·

My feet rise
off the planet,
pedal wheels of steel
that sparkle as
they spin me through
the open space I feel
winging out
to galaxies
far beyond the sun,
where bicycles
are satellites
their orbits never done.

—*Sandra Liatsos*

GOIN

G·PLACES

This song suggests the echoing of the mountains as the hikers sing. If you can't take a trip today, music can help you to travel in your imagination.

The Happy Wanderer

Music by Friedrich W. Möller
Words by Antonia Ridge

1. I love to go a - wan - der - ing,
2. I love to wan - der by the stream
3. I wave my hat to all I meet,
4. High o - ver - head, the sky - lark wing,

A - long the moun - tain track, And as I go,
That danc - es in the sun, So joy - ous - ly
And they wave back to me, And black - birds call
They nev - er rest at home, But just like me,

I love to sing, My knap - sack on my back.____
it calls to me, "Come! join my hap - py song."____
so loud and sweet From ev - ery green - wood tree.____
they love to sing, As o'er the world we roam.____

Refrain

Val - de - ri, Val - de - ra, Val - de - ri,

Val - de - ra ha ha ha ha ha, Val - de - ri,

Val - de - ra, My knap - sack on my back.____

You can take music with
you when you travel–in the car,
on a bus, bicycle riding, or even jogging.

**LISTEN to "Jubilee," and tell how the
singer traveled.**

Jubilee

Verse

Kentucky Play Party

1.   All   out   on   the   old   rail-road,   All   out   on   the   sea;
2.   Hard-est work   I   ev - er   done,   Work-ing   on   the   farm.
3.   If   I   had   no   horse   at   all,   I'd   be found a - crawl-in',
4.   Some will come on Sat-ur-day night,   Some will come on   Sun-day;

All   out   on   the   old rail-road,   Far   as   I   could   see.
Eas-i-est work   I   ev - er done was Swing-in' my true love's   arm.
Up   and down this   rock - y   road,   Look - in' for   my   dar-lin'.
If   you give 'em   half   a   chance,   They'll   be   back   on   Mon-day.

Refrain

Swing and turn,   Ju - bi-lee,   Live and learn,   Ju - bi-lee.

**SING "Jubilee." Pat with the beat on Lines 1 and 2.
Clap the rhythm of the words on Line 3.**

There are many ways to travel to the rhythms in music.

Try these. First walk the beat. Then jog by taking two steps to the beat. Finally, skate for two beats.

Walk   Walk   Walk   Walk

Jog- ging   Jog- ging   Jog- ging   Jog- ging

Skate   Skate

Greenland

SONGS TRAVEL, TOO!

Songs travel from place to place with the people who sing them. This sailing song traveled to North America from Europe.

NORTH AMERICA

Atlantic Ocean

LISTEN to "Turn the Glasses Over" and find places on the map that are included in the song.

Turn the Glasses Over

American Singing Game

I've been to Haarlem, I've been to Dover,
I've traveled this wide world all over,
Over, over, three times over,
Drink what you have to drink and turn the
    glasses over.
Sailing east, sailing west, Sailing o'er the ocean.
Better watch out when the boat begins to rock,
Or you'll lose your girl in the ocean.

LISTEN again, patting with the steady beat to find words that last for two beats.

DESIGNS IN MUSIC

Have you ever noticed train cars that are alike and different? Sometimes they make a design.

FIND the design made by the cars in this train. **What kind of car would come next?**

Many songs are designed using this pattern of same and different.

LISTEN to "Jubilee" to find its design. Point to the cars as you listen.

"Jubilee" is in **verse-refrain** form. Each **verse** has the same melody but different words. The **refrain** always has the same words and melody.

A VERSE-REFRAIN GAME

This game is about a vagabond, a person who travels from place to place. The game has the same verse-refrain form as "Jubilee."

LISTEN to the "Vagabond Game" as you pat the beat.

🎵 VAGABOND GAME

Verse:
My name is Amy, and I come from Alabama.
My name is Carlotta, and I come from California.
My name is Juan, and I come from Juarez.
My name is Miko, and I come from Mars.

Refrain:
As I went over the ocean,
As I went over the sea,
I came upon four vagabonds,
And this they said to me.

CREATE a verse to the "Vagabond Game" with three friends. Take turns saying a line of the verse, and then say the refrain together.

A VERSE-REFRAIN SONG

Here's a silly verse-refrain song. What verse in the song makes you smile?

Autumn to May

Words and Music
by Paul Stookey
and Peter Yarrow

Verse

1. Oh, once I had a lit-tle dog, his col-or it was brown.
2. Oh, once I had a ti-ny frog, he wore a vest of red.
3. Oh, once I had a flock of sheep, they grazed up-on a fea-ther;
4. Oh, once I had a down-y swan, she was so ver-y frail,

I taught him how to whis-tle, ___ to sing and dance and run,
He leaned up-on a sil-ver cane, a top hat on his head.
I'd keep them in a mu-sic box from wind and rain-y wea-ther,
She sat up-on an oys-ter shell and hatched me out a snail,

His legs they were four-teen yards long, his ears so ver-y wide,
He'd speak of far-off plac-es, of things to see and do,
And ev'-ry day the sun would shine, they'd fly all through the town
The snail it changed in-to a bird, the bird to but-ter-fly,

A - round the world in half   a day   up - on him   I could ride.
And all   the kings and queens he'd met while sail-ing   in   a   shoe.
To bring me back some gold - en rings and cand-y   by the pound.
And he who tells   a   big - ger "tail" would have to tell a lie.

Refrain

Sing tar-ry o   day,   Sing _____ Au-tumn to May. _____

LISTEN to "Autumn to May" again, singing on the refrain.

TRAVELING BY TRAIN

There are many
ways to travel. Some
ways are slower; some are
faster. Sometimes you can tell how
fast something is moving by listening.

THINK IT THROUGH

Describe how the sound of a train tells you
it's moving slower or faster.

In music, the speed of the beat can be slow or fast.
The speed of the beat is called **tempo.**

Meet STEVE REICH

*Steve Reich (b. 1936) was born in New York. He
composed the piece "Different Trains" to sound and feel
like a train traveling. First he recorded the voices of his
governess and a Pullman porter. He then mixed these
voices with string instruments and whistle sounds to
create a piece that sounds like a train moving.*

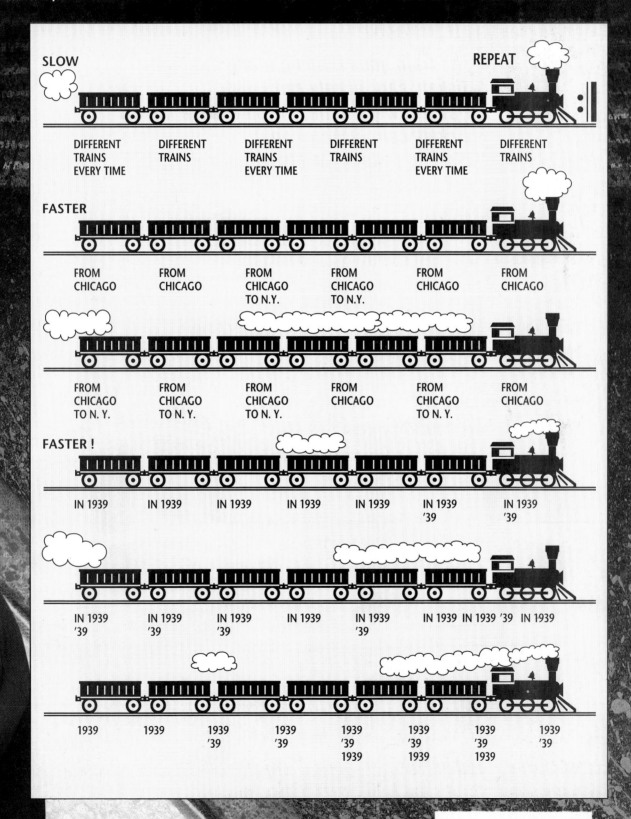

Different Trains *by Steve Reich*

LISTENING

LISTENING MAP *Follow this listening map as you listen to "Different Trains."*

SLOW
REPEAT

DIFFERENT TRAINS EVERY TIME | DIFFERENT TRAINS | DIFFERENT TRAINS EVERY TIME | DIFFERENT TRAINS | DIFFERENT TRAINS EVERY TIME | DIFFERENT TRAINS

FASTER

FROM CHICAGO | FROM CHICAGO | FROM CHICAGO TO N.Y. | FROM CHICAGO TO N.Y. | FROM CHICAGO | FROM CHICAGO

FROM CHICAGO TO N. Y. | FROM CHICAGO TO N. Y. | FROM CHICAGO TO N. Y. | FROM CHICAGO | FROM CHICAGO TO N. Y. | FROM CHICAGO

FASTER !

IN 1939 | IN 1939 | IN 1939 | IN 1939 | IN 1939 | IN 1939 '39 | IN 1939 '39

IN 1939 '39 | IN 1939 '39 | IN 1939 '39 | IN 1939 | IN 1939 '39 | IN 1939 IN 1939 '39 | IN 1939

1939 | 1939 | 1939 '39 | 1939 '39 | 1939 '39 1939 | 1939 '39 1939 | 1939 '39 1939 | 1939 '39

LISTEN to this speech piece to find what words sound like a passing train.

Jickety Can
Anonymous

The train goes running along the line.
Jickety can, jickety can,
I wish it were mine, I wish it were mine!
Jickety can, Jickety can.
Jickety, jickety, jickety can.

Say "Jickety Can" as if the train is leaving the station. How does the tempo change?

Musicians use the word **accelerando** to describe the tempo speeding up.

CREATE your own train music. Ask a partner to say "Jickety Can" as you speak your own train sounds in an eight-beat rhythm pattern.

MANCHESTER VALLEY

Joseph Pickett's painting of a train shows movement. Can you hear the *jickety can, jickety can* or *toot, toot* in this scene? What tempo and mood does the painting suggest?

TRAVELING RHYTHMS

Take a journey aboard a train in this folk song from Venezuela. You'll be traveling over bridges and through tunnels on your way to the capital.

LISTEN to "El tren" and brush your hands to the beat.

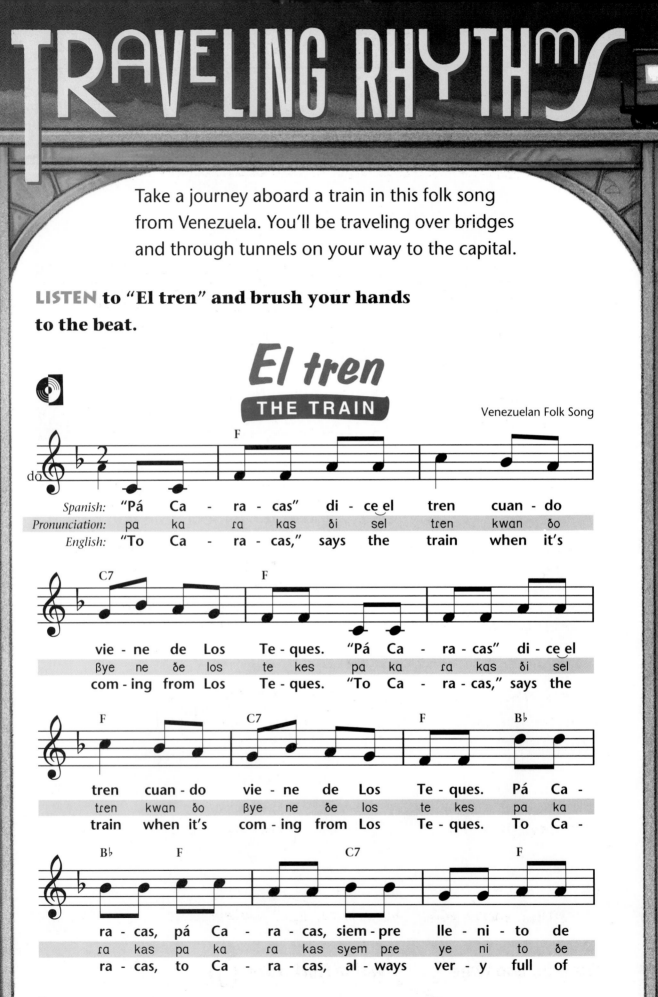

El tren
THE TRAIN

Venezuelan Folk Song

Spanish:	"Pá	Ca	-	ra	- cas"	di	- ce el	tren	cuan	- do
Pronunciation:	pɑ	ka		ɾa	kas	ði	sel	tɾen	kwɑn	ðo
English:	"To	Ca	-	ra	- cas,"	says	the	train	when	it's

vie	- ne	de	Los	Te	- ques.	"Pá	Ca	-	ra - cas"	di - ce el
βye	ne	ðe	los	te	kes	pa	ka		ɾa kas	ði sel
com	- ing	from	Los	Te	- ques.	"To	Ca	-	ra - cas,"	says the

tren	cuan - do	vie	- ne	de	Los	Te - ques.	Pá Ca -
tɾen	kwɑn ðo	βye	ne	ðe	los	te kes	pa ka
train	when it's	com	- ing	from	Los	Te - ques.	To Ca -

ra - cas,	pá	Ca	-	ra - cas,	siem - pre	lle - ni - to	de
ɾa kas	pa	ka		ɾa kas	syem pɾe	ye ni to	ðe
ra - cas,	to	Ca	-	ra - cas,	al - ways	ver - y	full of

78

gen - te   pa - sa a   ve - ces   por   un
xen   te   pa   sa   βe   ses   por   un
peo - ple,   some - times   pass - ing   through   a

tu - nel   y o - tras   ve - ces   por   un   puen - te.
tu   nel   yo   tras   βe   ses   por   un   pwen   te
tun - nel,   some - times   pass - ing   o - ver   bridg - es.

2. When it's going through a tunnel,
   it goes very, very slowly.
   (Repeat)

   Very gently, very slowly,
   so the people won't be frightened.
   (Repeat)

3. When it crosses over bridges,
   it begins to go much faster.
   (Repeat)

   Hurry, hurry, hurry, hurry,
   we're arriving in Caracas!
   (Repeat)

After your train ride, try reading a new traveling rhythm. The **tie** (⌣) tells you to hold the sound for two beats.

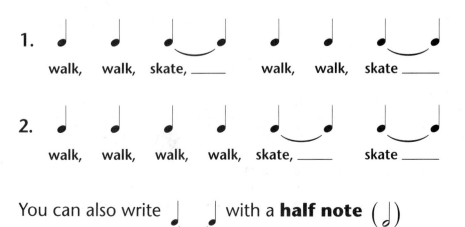

1. walk,   walk,   skate, ____   walk,   walk,   skate ____

2. walk,   walk,   walk,   walk,   skate, ____   skate ____

You can also write ♩⌣♩ with a **half note** (♩)

PAT with the beat as you say these rhythms.

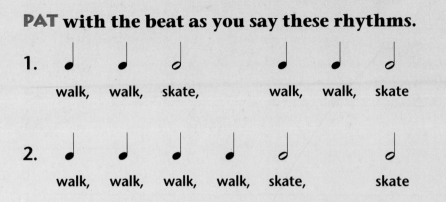

1.
walk,   walk,   skate,   walk,   walk,   skate

2.
walk,   walk,   walk,   walk,   skate,   skate

Find the line in "Turn the Glasses Over" that has both Rhythm 1 and Rhythm 2.

American Singing Game

Verse

I've   been   to   Haar - lem,   I've   been   to   Do - ver,

I've   trav - eled   this   wide   world   all   o - ver,

O - ver,   o - ver,   three   times   o - ver,

Drink   what   you   have   to   drink and   turn   the   glass - es   o - ver.

Refrain

Sail - ing   east,   sail - ing   west,   Sail - ing   o'er   the   o - cean,

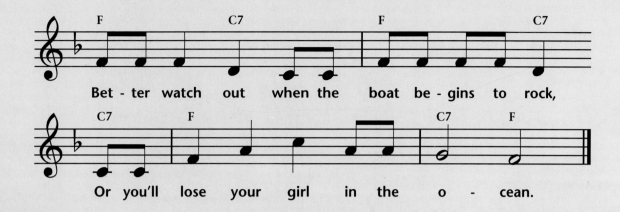

Bet - ter watch out when the boat be - gins to rock,

Or you'll lose your girl in the o - cean.

Find a partner and perform this movement called "wringing the dishrag."

Travel around the room with your partner as you listen to "Turn the Glasses Over." When you hear the words *turn the glasses over,* "wring the dishrag."

Take the Melody Up,

Have you ever traveled in a hot-air balloon? Take a melody up, up, and away by reading pitches higher than *do re mi*.

Look at the beginning of "Jubilee."

All out on the old rail-road, All out on the sea;

SING *old railroad.* **What pitch syllables are these notes?**

Are the other notes higher or lower than *do re mi?*

83

TWO PITCHES HIGHER THAN "MI"

The two pitches higher than *do re mi* in "Jubilee" are **so** and **la**.

do re mi   so la

What space is *so* in? What line is *la* on?

SING the first line of "Jubilee" and show the pitches with these movements.

la touch your head

so touch your shoulders

mi touch your waist

re touch your thighs

do touch your knees

SING "Deta, Deta" in Japanese.

Deta, Deta
THE MOON

Japanese
Children's Song
Collected and Transcribed by
Kathy B. Sorensen

2. Now the moon is hiding!
   Gone away, O gone away,
   Behind the clouds.
   Black as ink, behind the clouds.

Find *do* in "Deta, Deta." Then find *re mi so* and *la.*

SING "Deta, Deta" using pitch syllables
and movements.

TONE COLORS

Imagine you travel to the moon. Do you suppose the sounds would be the same as on Earth? Imagine how the tone colors of your voice and instruments might change.

Silver Moon *by Kitaro*

An electronic instrument called a **synthesizer** *can create and play many tone colors. Kitaro uses the synthesizer to write music. He imagined sounds of the moon and wrote a piece called "Silver Moon."*

LISTEN to "Silver Moon" and describe the tone colors. Move differently for each tone color.

How would you describe the mood or feeling of "Silver Moon"?

OF THE MOON

TONE COLOR WITH WORDS

If you wanted to write a poem about
"Silver Moon," you might write a haiku.

A *haiku* is a special kind of poem created
in Japan long ago. A haiku usually has 17
syllables! Many haiku are about nature.

READ this haiku and imagine the
scene it describes.

Clink, an iced branch falls.

I see the shattered moonlight

Scatter at my feet.

—KAZUE MIZUMURA

CREATE sounds with your voice to go
with the haiku.

PERFORM your vocal tone colors as
a friend reads the haiku.

What rhythm instruments could you use
to play with this haiku?

MOONLIGHT ON THE RIVER AT SEBA

The artist Hiroshige blends colors and images to
give his colored wood-block print a quiet, peaceful
tone. What instruments would you choose to reflect
the feeling of the art? Why?

SOUNDS OF TRAVELING

You can use your voice to make louder and softer sounds. Musicians know how loud or soft to play the music by signs called **dynamics.** Dynamics are written above or below the music.

p	soft
pp	softer
ppp	softest
f	loud
ff	louder
fff	loudest

Crescendo means to play or sing louder, little by little.

Decrescendo means to play or sing softer, little by little.

SAY "Jickety Can" following the dynamics above the lines.

f
The train goes running along the line.

p
Jickety can, jickety can

f
I wish it were mine. I wish it were mine!

p
Jickety can, jickety can

ppp _____ *fff*
Jickety, jickety, jickety can.

THINK IT THROUGH

Write the words to "Jickety Can" on a piece of paper and add your own dynamics. Say "Jickety Can" with your dynamics.

COMPARE the performances. Which do you like best? Why?

SPEAKING A CANON

These two trains are traveling at the same speed, but one started before the other.

SAY "Jickety Can" in two groups. One group starts before the other.

In music, this is called a **canon**.

LISTENING

Night Watch
by Anthony Holborne

LISTEN to "Night Watch," and move to show the dynamic changes you hear.

PICTURE YOUR TRAVELS

Do you take pictures or buy postcards when you travel? Pictures and postcards can help you to remember your trip.

Pictures can help you to remember songs, too. Try using the pictures on this page to remember all of the words to "Autumn to May."

NEW YORK, NY 100
PM
19 JA

LISTEN to "Autumn to May" and figure out the correct verse-refrain order for the pictures. Remember, the refrain will repeat four times, once after every verse.

SING TARRY O DAY SING AUTUMN TO MAY

SING "Autumn to May" and point to the pictures in the correct order.

95

**CLAP the rhythm below. Which sound takes up
two beat boxes?**

In this rhythm, the half notes and quarter
notes traveled to a new place.

CLAP this new rhythm.

CREATE your own eight-beat rhythm pattern.

Draw eight boxes, like the ones below, on a piece
of paper. Then, choose either a quarter note or a
half note to fill the boxes. Remember, a half note
takes two boxes.

**PERFORM your rhythms on
unpitched instruments.**

SOLVE THE MYSTERY!

This song is missing its melody. Use the rhythms below to tell what song it's from.

Which is the mystery song?

- "Autumn to May"
- "Jubilee"
- "Turn the Glasses Over"
- "Deta, Deta"

A RETURN TRIP

Take a musical journey by reviewing the songs you know. Begin by saying the refrain of the "Vagabond Game."

Refrain:
As I went over the ocean,
As I went over the sea,
I came upon four vagabonds,
And this they said to me.

Board a train in Venezuela as you sing "El tren."

Say the "Vagabond Game" refrain again, then sail on a clipper ship as you sing "Turn the Glasses Over."

Say the refrain again and then sing verse 2 of "Jubilee."

"Jubilee" is a verse-refrain song. What words start the refrain?

Finally, take a rest under the moon as you sing "Deta, Deta."

CHECK IT OUT

1. In which order do you hear the verse and refrain?

   a. refrain - verse - verse - refrain
   b. verse - refrain - verse - refrain
   c. verse - verse - refrain - refrain
   d. refrain - verse - refrain - verse

2. Which rhythm do you hear?

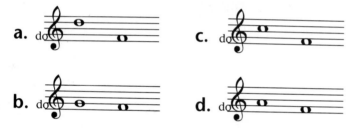

3. What pitches do you hear?

4. Which melody do you hear?

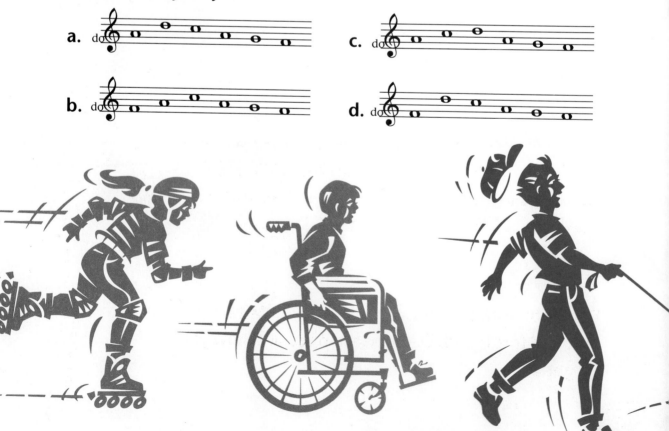

100

Make Your Own Traveling Melody

CLAP this rhythm. Say "walk" for ♩
"jogging" for ♫ and "skate" for ♩
Say nothing on 𝄽

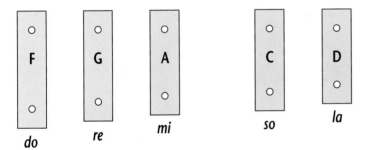

CREATE a melody for the rhythm using the
pitches *do re mi so* and *la*.

F	G	A	C	D
do	*re*	*mi*	*so*	*la*

Choose a partner and take turns playing each
other's melody.

**PERFORM your melodies in verse-refrain order.
One person plays his or her melody. Then the
class sings the refrain of "Jubilee." Repeat until
everyone's melody is played.**

Write

Decide on a place you would like to visit. Write a
postcard to a friend. Describe the place and how you
got there.

BUILT MY LADY A FINE BRICK HOUSE

Texas Folk Song

Built my la-dy a fine brick house, Built it in a gar-den;

I put her in but she jumped out, So fare thee well my dar-lin'!

HAUL AWAY, JOE

Sea Chantey

1. 'Way, haul a - way,_____ We'll
2. 'Way, haul a - way,_____ We'll

haul for fin - er weath - er,_____
haul a - way to - geth - er,_____

'Way, haul a - way,_____ Haul a - way, Joe.

El barquito
THE LITTLE BOAT

Panamanian Folk Song
English Version by MMH

Spanish: Ha-bía u-na vez un bar-co chi-qui-ti-to, _____

Pronunciation: a βyau na βes um baɾ ko chi ki ti to

English: Oh, once I had a pret-ty lit-tle sail-boat! _____

ha-bía u-na vez un bar-co chi-qui-ti-to, _____

a βyau na βes um baɾ ko chi ki ti to

Oh, once I had a pret-ty lit-tle sail-boat! _____

ha-bía u-na vez un bar-co chi-qui-ti-to, _____

a βyau na βes um baɾ ko chi ki ti to

Oh, once I had a pret-ty lit-tle sail-boat! _____

Que no po-dí-a, que no po-dí-a,

ke no po ði a ke no po ði a

A-las, it could not, a-las, it could not,

que no po-dí-a na-ve-gar.

ke no po ði a na βe gaɾ

a-las, it could not go to sea!

Pa-sa-ron u-na, dos, tres, cua-tro, cin-co,

pa sa ɾon u na ðos tres kwa tɾo sing ko

Well it was one, two, three, four, five, six, sev-en,

104

ENCORE

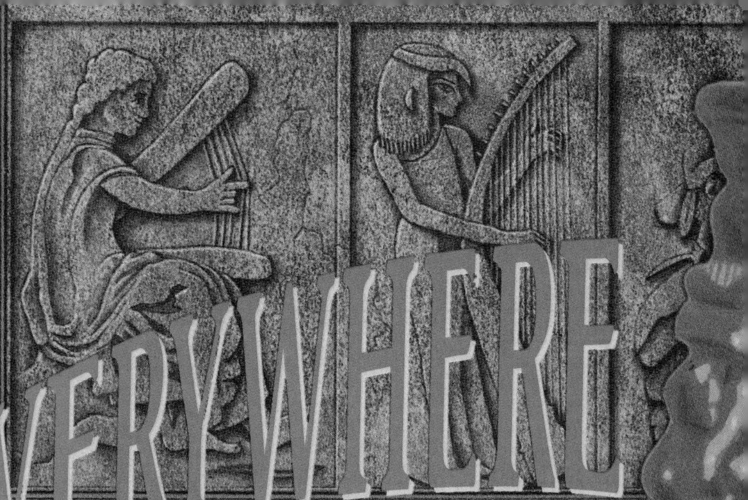

HARPS ARE EVERYWHERE

These pictures show harps from all over the world. How are the harps the same? How are they different?

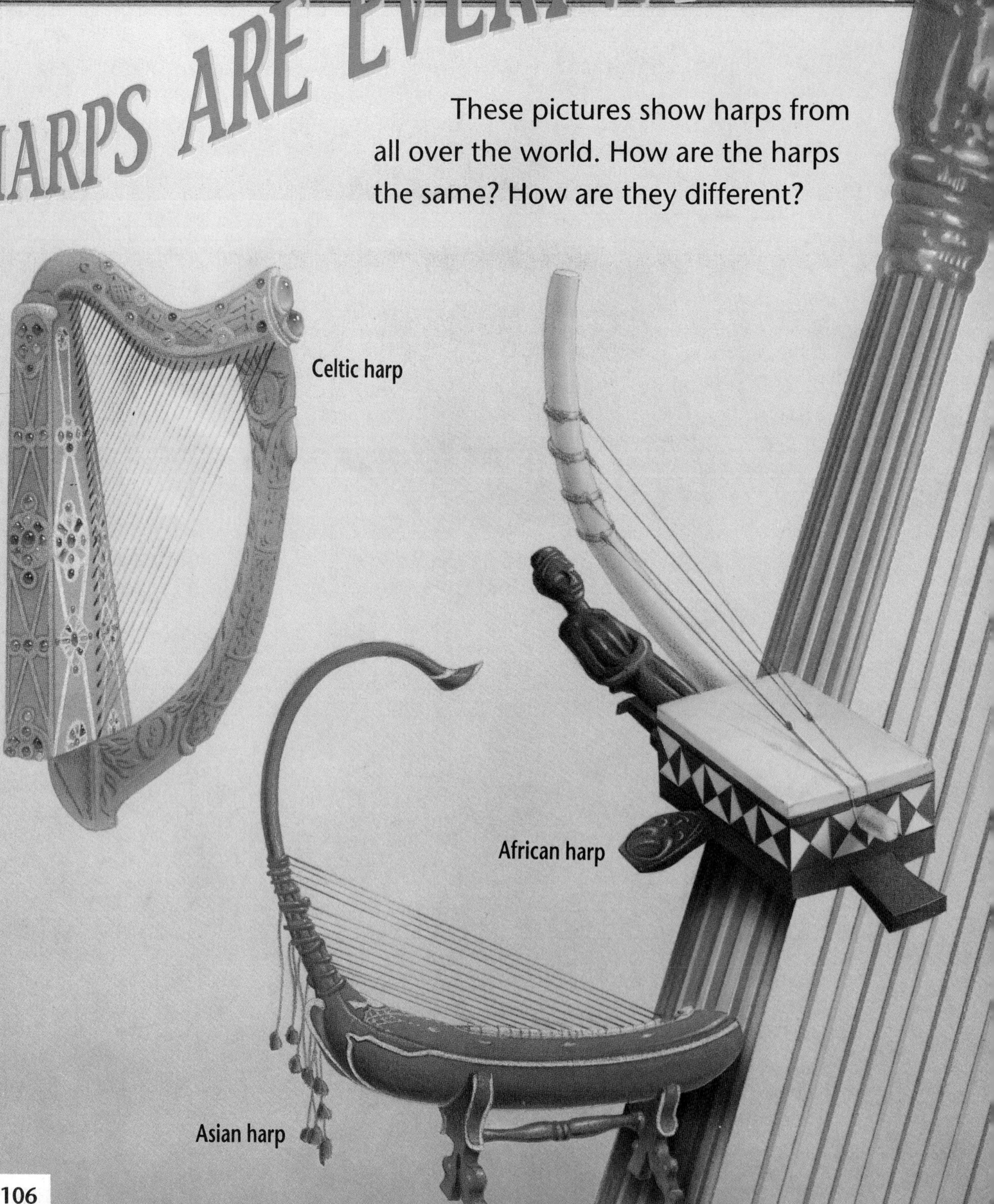
Celtic harp
African harp
Asian harp

The harp is one of the oldest instruments in the world and the oldest instrument in the string family. *Archeologists,* people who study ancient ways of life, have found pieces of harps in Egyptian tombs that are 5,000 years old!

European orchestral harp

MEET ALFREDO ROLANDO ORTIZ

Alfredo Rolando Ortiz borrowed a harp and took his first lesson from a friend. They were both 13 years old. Each week Ortiz carried his harp over many hills for his lesson. His parents did not think his interest would last, but he surprised them!

LISTEN to Alfredo Rolando Ortiz as he talks about his career as a harpist and plays *"El pajaro campana"* (The Bell Bird).

The harp can make many different sounds. The soft sounds of the harp have often reminded people of angels.

LISTEN to the sounds of the harp in this song.

Oh Lord, I Want Two Wings

African American Spiritual

1. Oh, Lord, I want two wings to cov - er my face, ___
2. Oh, Lord, I want two gold - en shoes for my feet, ___
3. Oh, Lord, I want a gold - en harp ___ to play, ___

Oh, Lord, I want two wings to cov - er my face, ___
Oh, Lord, I want two gold - en shoes for my feet, ___
Oh, Lord, I want a gold - en harp ___ to play, ___

Oh, Lord, I want two wings to cov - er my face, ___
Oh, Lord, I want two gold - en shoes for my feet, ___
Oh, Lord, I want a gold - en harp ___ to play, ___

And the world can do me no harm. ___

EVERYDAY MUSIC

THE WORLD IS
DAY-BREAKING

What are days for?

Days are where we live.

They come, they wake us

Time and time over.

They are to be happy in:

Where can we live but days?

—*Sekiya Miyoshi*

The poem on page 111 invites us to enjoy our everyday lives. Singing is a great way to appreciate the gift of each new day.

Who Will Buy?

Words and Music
by Lionel Bart

1., 2. Who will buy this won-der-ful morn - ing?
3. Who will buy this won-der-ful feel - ing?

Such a sky you nev-er did see.____
I'm so high, I swear I could fly.____

Who will tie it up with a rib -
Me, oh, my, I don't want to lose____

3rd time to Coda ⊕ F

- bon And put it in a box for me?
— it, so what am I to do, to

EVERYDAY FOLK MUSIC

Many of the songs you sing every day were first sung hundreds of years ago. If we don't know who created them, they're called **folk songs.** Some folk songs tell stories. The folk song "Charlie" comes from the British Isles. It tells about "Bonnie Prince Charlie," who tried to claim the British throne in 1745.

Charlie

Adapted from a British Folk Song

1. Step her to your weev'ly wheat, and step her to your barley,
   Step her to you weev'ly wheat to bake a cake for Charlie.

   Refrain
   Over the river to feed my sheep, Over the river, Charlie!
   Over the river to feed my sheep, And measure up my barley!

2. Over and over, ten times over, Charlie is a rover;
   Take your partner by the hands and wring the dishrag over.

   Refrain

Here's another piece that tells about an everyday event–making a favorite food! You might hear this game on playgrounds in Texas, Mexico, and Ecuador. It tells about a chocolate sauce called *mole*. The sauce is served with rice, tomatoes, chicken, and chili peppers.

CLAP the rhythm of the words to find a line that has the same rhythm as *Bate, bate, chocolate.*

BATE, BATE

Mexican Game

Bate, bate, chocolate,
Con arroz y con tomate.
Uno, dos, tres, CHO-,
Uno, dos, tres, CO-,
Uno, dos, tres, LA-,
Uno, dos, tres, TE,
Chocolate,
Chocolate,
Chocolate,
Chocolate.

EQUAL AND UNEQUAL RHYTHMS

"Charlie" and "Bate, bate" are both performed to a steady beat, but the rhythm of the words sounds and feels different. Find out why.

CLAP the rhythm of the words in "Bate, bate."

Ba- te, ba- te, cho- co- la- te,
■■■ ■■■ ■■■ ■■■ ■■■ ■■■ ■■■ ■■■

CLAP the rhythm of the words in "Charlie."

Step   her to   your weev'- ly wheat and
■■■   ■■■ ■■■   ■■■ ■■■   ■■■ ■■■   ■■■

COMPARE the rhythms of the words. Which rhythm has two unequal (long-short) sounds to each beat? Two equal (short-short) sounds to each beat?

The folk song "Veinte y tres" comes from sheepherders in New Mexico.

LISTEN to "Veinte y tres" and pat the rhythm of the words.

U-   na‿y U-   na‿y U-   na‿y U   na‿y
▬▬▬ ▬ ▬▬▬ ▬ ▬▬▬ ▬ ▬▬▬ ▬

Is the rhythm of "Veinte y tres" equal or unequal?

SONG SHAPES

Some folk songs are created from the words of everyday games.

LISTEN to "Rocky Road" and find the words *red light, green light.* Can you find another game in this song?

Rocky Road

Based on Lyrics Adapted and Arranged by
Peter Yarrow, Paul Stookey, and Albert Grossman

Verse 1: Red light, green light, 'round the town,
Found a penny on the ground,
Met a friend I never knowed,
Walkin' down old Rocky Road.

Refrain: Red, green, old Rocky Road,
Tell me what you see,
Red, green, old Rocky Road,
Tell me what you see,
Tell me inside out, Tell me upside down,
All around the block, all around the town.

Verse 2: Hey, Jimmy Higgins your name's been called,
Come and stand behind the wall.
Red light, green light, come and play,
Little Miss Jenny, you're it today.   *Refrain*

Ending: One p'tato, two p'tato, three p'tato, four,
Cross the line, close the door.

Tracing the shape of the melody can help you to learn
a new song.

**TRACE the shape of this part of "Rocky Road"
when you hear it.**

119

For hundreds of years people had to get water from wells by drawing it up in a bucket. The folk song "Draw a Bucket of Water" tells of this everyday chore. It comes from the Georgia Sea Islands.

SING the first part of the song as you pretend to pull a bucket of water from the well. Sing the ending as if you are surprised!

Draw a Bucket of Water

African American
Singing Game

Refrain: Draw a bucket of water
For my only daughter.

1. There's none in the bunch, we're all out the bunch,
   You go under, sister Sally. *Refrain*
2. There's one in the bunch, and three out the bunch,
   You go under, sister Sally. *Refrain*
3. There's two in the bunch, and two out the bunch,
   You go under, sister Sally. *Refrain*
4. There's three in the bunch, and one out the bunch,
   You go under, sister Sally.
Ending: Frog in the bucket and I can't get him out.
   Repeat 8 times

TRACE the shape of the melody of "Draw a Bucket of Water," and match the shape to one of the patterns below.

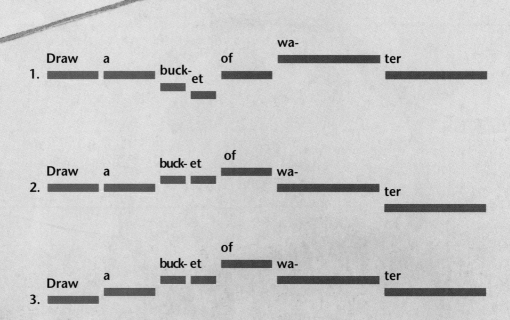

Conducting Too!

Sometimes folk songs like "Draw a Bucket of Water" are performed while working. The movements become part of the song.

PERFORM the movements for "Draw a Bucket of Water" as you sing the song.

You'll pretend to pull water out of the well, make a bucket with your friends, and act surprised at what's in the bucket besides water!

122

You can be the conductor! First practice by patting with the beat as you listen to this speech piece.

Rattlesnake Skipping Song

Mississauga rattlesnakes **Eat** brown bread.
Mississauga rattlesnakes **Fall** down dead.
If you catch a caterpillar, **Feed** him apple juice; But
If you catch a rattlesnake, **Turn** him loose!

—*Dennis Lee*

CONDUCT in sets of two as you listen again. Think *one* on the strong beat, the downbeat, and *two* on the weak beat, the upbeat.

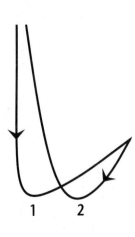

1   2

Arcangelo Corelli

The Granger Collection

Arcangelo Corelli (1653–1713) lived in Italy about three hundred years ago. He loved to play the violin, and he wrote music for many different instruments. The king and queen invited Corelli to live in the royal palace, where he wrote and played music just for them.

LISTENING

Gigue (excerpt) from Sonata for Violin and Continuo
by Arcangelo Corelli

LISTENING MAP *Now it's time to conduct the orchestra. Show the beats or tap on the pictures below as you listen to this music.*

Pat Me a Song

In an unequal rhythm, one sound is long and one sound is short. In the rhythm below, the first sound is longer than the second.

♩ ♪♪ ♪

FIND this quarter-eighth pattern in "Veinte y tres."

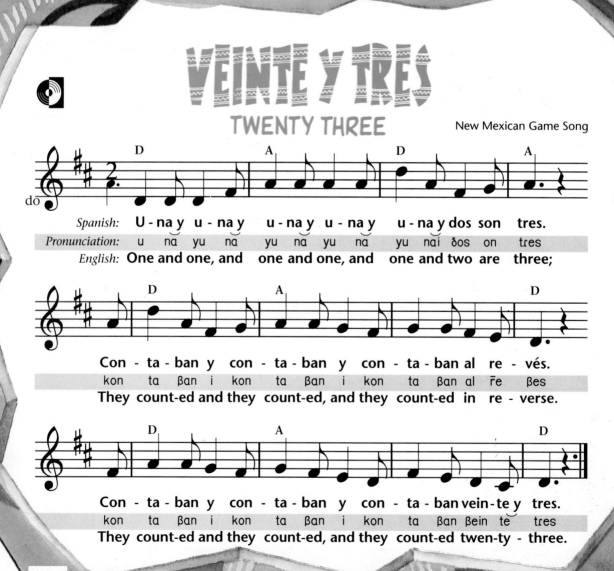

VEINTE Y TRES
TWENTY THREE

New Mexican Game Song

D   A   D   A

Spanish: U - na y u - na y   u - na y u - na y   u - na y dos son   tres.
Pronunciation: u nā yu nā   yu nā yu nā   yu nāi ðos on   tres
English: One and one, and   one and one, and   one and two are   three;

D   A   D

Con - ta - ban y con - ta - ban y con - ta - ban al re - vés.
kon ta βan i kon ta βan i kon ta βan al r̄e βes
They count-ed and they count-ed, and they count-ed in re - verse.

D   A   D

Con - ta - ban y con - ta - ban y con - ta - ban vein-te y tres.
kon ta βan i kon ta βan i kon ta βan βein te tres
They count-ed and they count-ed, and they count-ed twen-ty - three.

126

CHARLIE'S BACK!

You can find the quarter-eighth pattern many times in this song.

CLAP the rhythm of "Charlie."

Step her to your weev'-ly wheat, and step her to your bar - ley,

Step her to your weev'-ly wheat to bake a cake for Char - lie.

Find the places where the quarter-eighth pattern stops.

The note above these words is a **dotted quarter note** (♩.) In "Charlie," the dotted quarter note gets the beat. The meter sign (²⁄₈·) at the beginning of the song tells you that there are two beats in each measure.

bar - ley, Char - lie.

A beat with no sound in $\frac{2}{\cdot}$ meter is called a **dotted quarter rest** (𝄽·)

CLAP this pattern.

Take turns playing the pattern on a tambourine as your class sings "Charlie."

CHARLIE

Adapted from a British Folk Song

Verse

1. Step her to your weev'-ly wheat, and step her to your bar-ley,
2. O-ver and o-ver, ten times o - ver, Char-lie is a ro-ver;

Step her to your weev'-ly wheat to bake a cake for Char - lie.
Take your part-ner by the hands and wring the dish-rag o - ver.

Refrain

O-ver the riv-er to feed my sheep, O-ver the riv - er, Char - lie!

O-ver the riv-er to feed my sheep, And mea-sure up my bar - ley!

CLAP these rhythms in ⅔ meter.

1.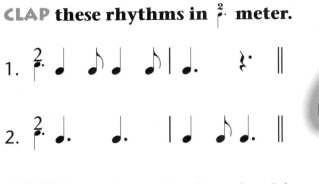

2. (rhythm notation)

LISTEN for these rhythms in this song.

Row, Row, Row Your Boat
Traditional Round

Row, row, row your boat
Gently down the stream;
Merrily, merrily, merrily, merrily,
Life is but a dream.

Which rhythm matches *Row, row, row your boat?*
Gently down the stream?
Life is but a dream?

THINK IT THROUGH

Use the two rhythms above to create a speech piece. Choose words to say with the rhythms. Perform your pieces with classroom instruments.

TWO NEW PITCHES IN THE WELL

In this song, you'll find two new pitches.

FIND the pitches *do re* and *mi* as you listen and trace the first line of "Draw a Bucket of Water."

do Draw a buck-et of wa- ter, For my on- ly daugh- ter.
ter.

The two new pitches you found are called low *la* and low *so*. In this song, low *so* is on a **ledger line**, a line added below the staff.

do
so₁ la₁ do re mi

You also found a curved line called a slur. A **slur** (⌣) tells you to sing a syllable on more than one pitch.

Find a slur over the word *daughter*.

DRAW A BUCKET OF WATER

African American Play-Party Song

1.–4. Draw a buck-et of wa - ter For my on - ly daugh - ter.

There's
{ none in the bunch, we're all out the bunch,
one in the bunch, and three out the bunch,
two in the bunch, and two out the bunch,
three in the bunch, and one out the bunch, }

(Four times)

You ___ go un - der, sis - ter Sal - ly.

Faster

Frog in the buck - et and I can't get him out,

Frog in the buck - et and I can't get him out,

Frog in the buck - et and I can't get him out,

Frog in the buck - et and I can't get him out.

Written and adapted by Bessie Jones. Collected and Edited by Alan Lomax. TRO - © Copyright 1972 Ludlow Music, Inc., New York, NY. Used by permission.

"Draw a Bucket of Water" and "Now Let Me Fly" were first sung by enslaved Africans brought to America to work. "Now Let Me Fly" is a religious folk song called a **spiritual.** Imagine being forced to work all day in a large field under a hot sun. Why might you sing "Now Let Me Fly"?

Now Let Me Fly

African American Spiritual

Refrain

Now let me fly,——— Now let me fly,——— Now let me fly—— way up high,— Way in the mid-dle of the air.

Verse

Way down yon-der in the mid-dle of the field,

See me work-ing at the char-i-ot wheel.

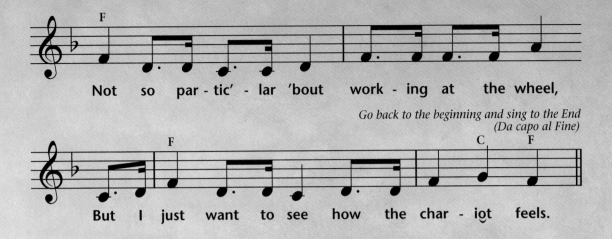

Not so par-tic'-lar 'bout work-ing at the wheel,

Go back to the beginning and sing to the End
(Da capo al Fine)

But I just want to see how the char-iot feels.

CREATE your own melody for the verse of "Now Let Me Fly." Use these pitches.

la

so

mi

re

do

la₁

so₁

133

For many years most folk songs were not written down.
Instead, they were passed from singer to singer. People
often changed the songs a little each time they sang
them. For this reason, many folk songs have come
down to us in different versions. Here are two versions
of the song "Charlie."

SING "Charlie" with an unequal rhythm
in ²/⁴. meter.

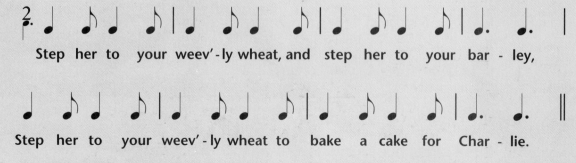

Step her to your weev'-ly wheat, and step her to your bar - ley,

Step her to your weev'-ly wheat to bake a cake for Char - lie.

ARLIES"

Now try "Charlie" a different way!

SING "Charlie" with an equal rhythm in $\frac{2}{4}$ meter.

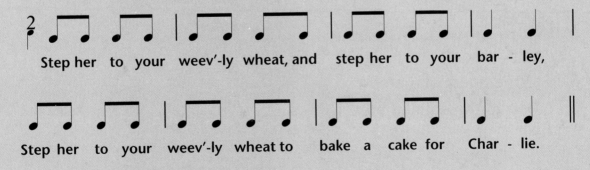

Step her   to   your   weev'-ly   wheat,   and   step   her   to   your   bar - ley,

Step her   to   your   weev'-ly   wheat   to   bake   a   cake   for   Char - lie.

THINK IT THROUGH

How does the $\frac{2}{4}$ meter make the song feel different?
How would you move differently when the song is
in $\frac{2}{4}$ meter?

LISTENING

Sentry Box

and

Andrew and His Cutty Gun

Traditional Fife and Drum Music

Fife and drum music has a lively rhythm. This music was often played to help soldiers march together. Today, you can hear it in parades.

PAT each rhythm as you listen to these two pieces.

COMPARE the two pieces.

Which one feels like it is in equal meter? In unequal meter?

MOVE to show the meters.

Skip to the unequal meter. Step-hop to the equal meter.

You can step-hop or skip to "Bate, bate," too!

MOVE to "Bate, bate" in equal $\left(\begin{smallmatrix}2\\4\end{smallmatrix}\right)$ meter, then in unequal $\left(\begin{smallmatrix}2\\4\end{smallmatrix}\cdot\right)$ meter.

BATE, BATE

Mexican Game

**Bate, bate, chocolate,
Con arroz y con tomate,
Uno, dos, tres, CHO-,
Uno, dos, tres, CO-,
Uno, dos, tres, LA-,
Uno, dos, tres, TE,
Chocolate, Chocolate,
Chocolate, Chocolate.**

Match these rhythms in $\begin{smallmatrix}2\\4\end{smallmatrix}\cdot$ to a line of "Bate, bate."

ROAD SIGNS

In this song the phrase *Red, green, old Rocky Road, Tell me what you see* repeats. A **repeat sign** (𝄆 𝄇) tells you to repeat this phrase of the song.

FIND the repeat signs in "Rocky Road," and then sing the song.

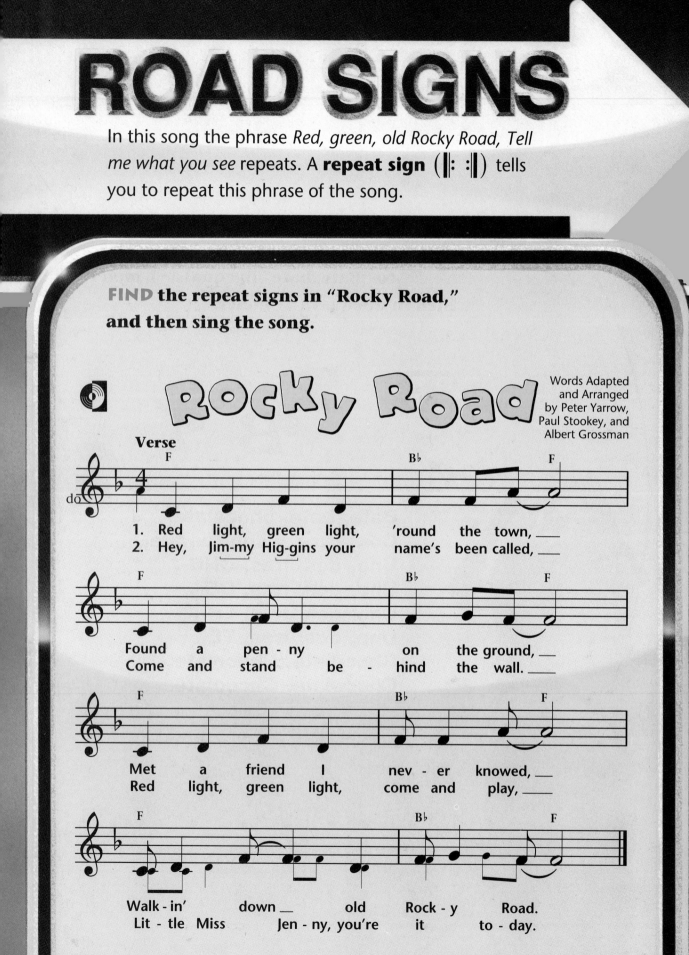

Rocky Road

Words Adapted and Arranged by Peter Yarrow, Paul Stookey, and Albert Grossman

Verse

1. Red light, green light, 'round the town, ___
2. Hey, Jim-my Hig-gins your name's been called, ___

Found a pen - ny on the ground, ___
Come and stand be - hind the wall. ___

Met a friend I nev - er knowed, ___
Red light, green light, come and play, ___

Walk - in' down ___ old Rock - y Road.
Lit - tle Miss Jen - ny, you're it to - day.

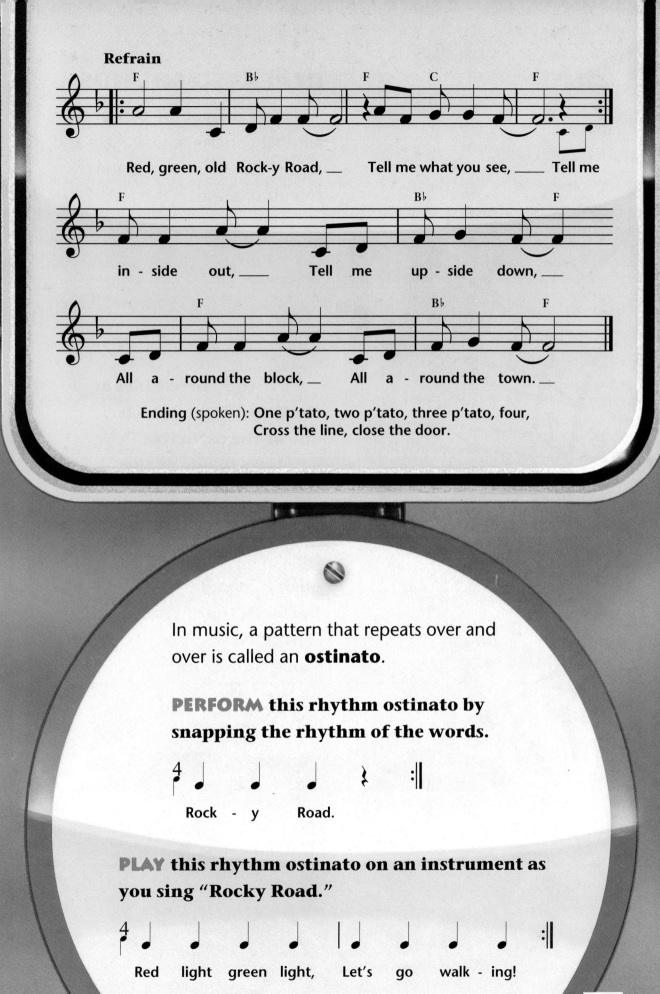

Refrain

Red, green, old Rock-y Road, __ Tell me what you see, ____ Tell me

in - side out, ____ Tell me up - side down, __

All a - round the block, __ All a - round the town. __

Ending (spoken): One p'tato, two p'tato, three p'tato, four,
Cross the line, close the door.

In music, a pattern that repeats over and over is called an **ostinato**.

PERFORM this rhythm ostinato by snapping the rhythm of the words.

Rock - y Road.

PLAY this rhythm ostinato on an instrument as you sing "Rocky Road."

Red light green light, Let's go walk - ing!

REPEATED SOUNDS

Are there rides at the park or the fair that you like to ride again and again? Can you imagine the sounds of these rides?

LISTENING

Three Rides at the Park *by Linda Williams*

LISTEN to "Three Rides at the Park." Match each one of the ostinatos you hear to one of the three rides pictured.

CREATE a movement for each ostinato with a friend. Perform your movements as you listen again.

You can sing an ostinato, too! A short melody that repeats over and over is called a **melodic ostinato.**

SING this melodic ostinato and follow the repeat sign.

Ostinato

Way in the mid-dle of the air.

Take turns singing the ostinato as your class sings "Now Let Me Fly."

SING!
High, Low, and In Between

SING the refrain of "Now Let Me Fly."

Sing way down low,

Now   let me   fly, _____

way up high,

Now   let me   fly, _____

and way in the middle of the air.

Now   let me   fly __   way up high, __ Way in the mid-dle of the   air.

SING the refrain again using pitch syllables.

Name the pitches in the tinted measures.

SING the refrain of **"Now Let Me Fly" again.**

Hold your hands on the floor when you sing low *so*.

so₁

Hold your hands above your head when you sing *so*.

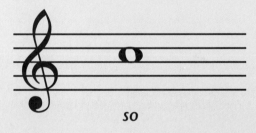

so

Hold your hands on your waist when you sing *do*.

do

Play a game of "Musical Red Light" and freeze to show which pitch you hear.

MISSING PITCHES

Charlie lost some notes from his song. Help Charlie find the missing notes.

	Step	her	to	your	weev'-	ly	wheat	to	bake	a	cake	for	Char -	lie.
	do	*do*	*do*	*re*	*mi*	*so*	*mi*	*re*	*?*	*?*	*?*	*?*	*?*	*?*

Use these pitch stairs to help you name the missing pitches.

la

so

mi

re

do

la,

so,

SONGS FOR EVERY DAY

Match these song titles to the pictures.

"Charlie"

"Bate, bate"

"Rocky Road"

"Draw a Bucket of Water"

"Veinte y tres"

Make up a silly story that includes all of these song titles. Start your story this way:

One day I went to "Draw a Bucket of Water" from the well when . . .

or

I was making popcorn when my friend "Charlie" said . . .

Read the story and sing the songs when you come to their titles.

146

CHECK IT OUT

1. Which of these has an equal rhythm?

   a.   b.   c.

2. Which of these has an unequal rhythm?

   a.   b.   c.

3. Which rhythm do you hear?

4. Choose the pitches you hear.

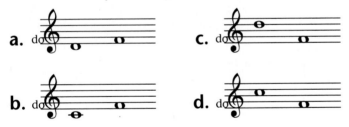

5. Which melody do you hear?

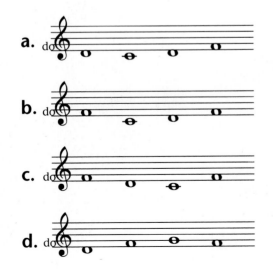

148

CREATE

Make Your Own Everyday Music

Combine some movements to make your own eight-beat pattern. Draw these lines on a piece of paper.

Rhythm   ____ ____ | ____ ____ | ____ ____ | ____ ____ ‖

Movement   ____ ____   ____ ____   ____ ____   ____ ____

Put one of these on each line.

Rhythm
Movement   **walk**   **skip - ping**   **rest**

Use the bells *so, la, do re mi so la* to add a melody. Begin and end on *do* (F).

C   D   F   G   A   C   D

so,   *la,*   *do*   *re*   *mi*   *so*   *la*

PLAY your melody while others perform your movement pattern.

Write

Many folk songs are based on everyday events. Write about an everyday event that might make a good folk song.

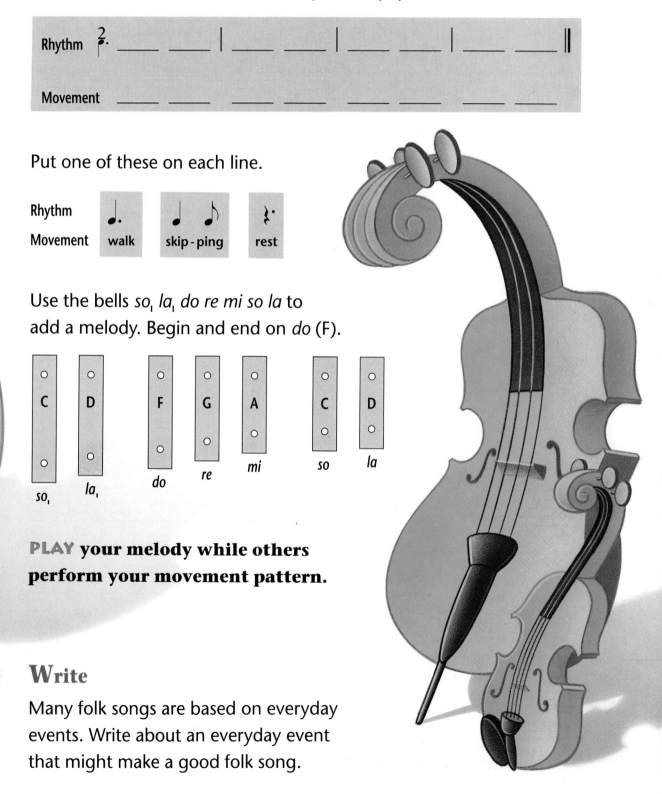

Treasure Chests

Words and Music by Minnie O'Leary

Verse

1. Some of us come from a dis-tant land, Some of us from near-
2. Treas-ures come from _ years a-go from coun - tries far a-
3. Hol-i-days, games and _ stor - ies, Lan-gua-ges and ___

by, But all of us car-ry a treas-ure chest With
way, _____ Treas-ures come from our fam - i - lies, Last
songs; _____ Faith _ and cour-age and wis - dom, And

things that gold can't buy; with things that gold can't buy.
year or yes - ter - day; last year or yes - ter - day.
ways to get a - long; and ways to get a - long.

Refrain

And when we share our treas-ure chests we

all grow rich, you see. The rich-es in that treas-ure chest are

what makes you and me; are what makes you and me.

Frère Jacques
Are You Sleeping?

French Folk Song
Traditional English Words

French: Frè - re Jac - ques, Frè - re Jac - ques,
Pronunciation: frɛ rə ʒɑ kə frɛ rə ʒɑ kə
English: Are you sleep - ing, are you sleep - ing,

Dor - mez - vous, dor - mez - vous?
dɔr me vu dɔr me vu
Broth - er John, Broth - er John?

Son - nez les ma - ti - nes, son - nez les ma - ti - nes,
sɔ ne le mɑ ti nə sɔ ne le mɑ ti nə
Morn-ing bells are ring - ing, morn-ing bells are ring - ing,

Din, dan, don, din, dan, don.
dɛ̃ dɑ̃ dɔ̃ dɛ̃ dɑ̃ dɔ̃
Ding, ding, dong, ding, ding, dong.

Golden Ring Around the Susan Girl

Southern Appalachian Folk Song
New Words and Music by Jean Ritchie

Verse   F

1. Gold - en ring a - round the Su - san girl,
2. Do - si - do right, you Su - san girl,
3. Hand over hand, you Su - san girl,
(4.) take 'im on home, Su - san girl,

F   C 7

Gold - en ring a - round the Su - san girl,
Do - si - do right, you Su - san girl,
Hand over hand, you Su - san girl,
Take 'im on home, Su - san girl,

F

Gold - en ring a - round the Su - san girl,
Do - si - do right, you Su - san girl,
Hand over hand, you Su - san girl,
Take 'im on home, Su - san girl,

F   C 7   F

All the way a - round the Su - san girl. _____
All the way a - round the Su - san girl. _____ And
All the way a - round the Su - san girl. _____
All the way a - round the Su - san girl. _____ Then

F

Take a lit - tle girl and give 'er a whirl,
do - si - do left, you Su - san girl,
Get a lit - tle fas - ter, Su - san girl,
take 'im on home, Su - san girl,

Take a lit - tle girl and give 'er a whirl,
Do - si - do left, you Su - san girl,
Get a lit - tle fas - ter, Su - san girl,
Take 'im on home, Su - san girl,

Take a lit - tle girl and give 'er a whirl,
Do - si - do left, you Su - san girl,
Get a lit - tle fas - ter, Su - san girl,
Take 'im on home, Su - san girl,

All the way a - round the Su - san girl.

Refrain

'Round and a - round, Su - san girl, 'Round and a - round,

Su - san girl, 'Round and a - round, Su - san girl,

All the way a - round the Su - san girl.

4. Then

VOICES FROM THE HEART

Many Native American songs celebrate the events of everyday life. They also remind people to respect one another and the things of nature. The songs praise what is important in the hearts of the people and in their culture. Listen to songs from the Hopi, the Santa Clara Pueblo, and the Lakota Nations.

LISTENING Hopi Lullaby

In the Hopi culture, aunts, uncles, and grandparents help the mother and father take care of the children. Listen to a lullaby about two little stink bugs.

LISTENING Pueblo Corn Grinding Song

Corn is an important crop among the Pueblo groups. Listen to a song that women from Santa Clara Pueblo sing while they grind corn.

154

Lakota Honor Song

LISTENING

*Honoring songs are an important part
of the Indian tradition. These songs
recognize special achievements. People
are honored for the help they give the
community. Older people are honored
for the useful experience they can pass on.
This song honors all Lakotas who fought
for the United States.*

**DESCRIBE the voice of the singer.
Is it high or low?**

Encore **155**

Mohawk basket

dress moccasins

VISUAL ARTS

Traditionally, Native Americans made many of their everyday objects. Hopi women, for example, made beautiful pottery and baskets that were used as trays, serving platters, and containers for corn.

Hopi pottery

Lakota woman's traditional buckskin dress

Modern Native American artists often combine traditional Indian art with other forms of art. Sculptors carve figures and other objects from stone or other materials. Other artists paint pictures.

Oscar Howe, a Lakota, was a painter. Sometimes he used traditional Native American dances in his work. In *Dance of the Double Woman,* he used many shapes and colors.

Stanley Hill, a Mohawk, is famous for his moose antler carvings. The eagle is respected by many Native Americans.

ALPHABET
Stew

Words can be stuffy, as sticky as glue,
but words can be tutored to tickle you too,
to rumble and tumble and tingle and sing,
to buzz like a bumblebee, coil like a spring.

Juggle their letters and jumble their sounds,
swirl them in circles and stack them in mounds,
twist them and tease them and turn them about,
teach them to dance upside down, inside out.

Make mighty words whisper and tiny words roar
in ways no one ever had thought of before;
cook an improbable alphabet stew,
and words will reveal little secrets to you.

—*Jack Prelutsky*

THAT SING

SWINGING ON A STAR

Words and Music by Johnny Burke
and James Van Heusen

Swing

Refrain   Gm7

Would you like to swing on a

C7   F7

star,   Car - ry moon - beams home in a

B♭   G7   C7

jar, _____ And be bet - ter off than you are,

F7   B♭

Or would you rath - er be a (1.) mule?   A
                                            (2.) pig?   A
                                            (3.) fish?   A

Verse
B♭   E♭   B♭

mule is an an - i - mal with   long fun - ny ears, He
pig   is an an - i - mal with   dirt on his face, His
fish won't do an - y - thing but swim in a brook, He

B♭   E♭   B♭

kicks up at an - y - thing he   hears. _____ His
shoes are a ter - ri - ble dis - grace. _____ He's
can't write his name or read a book. _____ To

160

C7
back   is   brawn - y   and   his   brain   is   weak,____   He's
got   no   man - ners   when   he   eats   his   food.____   He's
fool   the   peo - ple   is   his   on - ly   thought,____   And

C7   **F**   **F7**
just   plain   stu - pid   with   a   stub - born   streak.   And   by   the
ve - ry   la - zy   and   ex - treme - ly   rude.   But   if   you
though   he's   slip - per - y,   he   still   gets   caught.   But   then   if

B♭   **E♭**   **B♭**
way,   if   you   hate   to   go   to   school,
don't   care   a   feath - er   or   a   fig,
that   sort   of   life   is   what   you   wish,

F7   **1., 2.**   **B♭**
You   may   grow   up   to   be   a   mule.____ }   Or   would   you
You   may   grow   up   to   be   a   pig.____
You   may   grow   up   to   be

3.   **B♭**   **G7**
fish.____   And   all   the   mon - keys   aren't   in   the

C7   **F7**   **B♭**
zoo,   Ev - 'ry   day   you   meet   quite   a   few.____   So   you

G7   **C7**   **F7**
see   it's   all   up   to   you.   You   can   be   bet - ter   than   you

D7   Gm   Cm   **F7**   **B♭**
are.   You   could   be   swing - ing   on   a   star.____

SIMPLY SILLY STORY SONGS

SING this silly story song as you tap with the beat.

FROG WENT A-COURTIN'

Kentucky Folk Song
Additional Words by MMH

Verse

Dm

1. Frog went a-court-in' and he did ride.
(2.) rode right ___ to ___ Miss Mous-ie's door,
(3.) took Miss ___ Mous-ie on his knee,
(4.) out my ___ Un-cle Rat's con-sent,
5. Un-cle Rat ___ laughed ___ and shook his sides,

G   F   G

Rink - tum bod - y min - chy cam - bo.

Dm

Sword and buck-ler by his side,
Found Miss Mous-ie sweep-in' the floor.
And said, "Miss Mous-ie, will you mar-ry me?"
I could not mar-ry the pres-i-dent."
To think his niece would be a bride.

162

Rink - tum bod - y min - chy cam - bo.

Refrain

Ki - man-ee - ro down to Cai - ro, Ki - man-ee - ro Cai - ro.

Shad-dle - ad - dle - ad - a - ba - ba, lad - da - ba - ba link - tum.

Rink - tum bod - y min - chy cam - bo.

2. He
3. He
4. "With -

6. Who will make the wedding gown?
Old Miss Rat from Pumpkin Town.

7. Where will the wedding supper be?
Way down yonder in a hollow tree.

8. What will the wedding supper be?
A fried mosquito and a black-eyed pea.

9. First to come was a bumblebee,
He set his fiddle on his knee.

10. Next to come was a doodle bug,
Carrying a water jug.

11. Next to come was a flying moth;
She laid out the tablecloth.

12. Next to come was an itty-bitty flea
To dance a jig for the bumblebee.

13. Next to come was a big old cow;
She wanted to dance but she
didn't know how.

14. Next to come was a big black snake;
He ate up all the wedding cake.

15. Last to come was an old gray cat;
She swallowed up the mouse and
ate up the rat.

16. Mr. Frog went hopping over the
brook;
A duck came along and swallowed
him up.

17. Now is the end of him and her;
Guess there won't be no
tadpoles covered with fur!

18. Little piece of cornbread lying on
the shelf,
If you want any more you can sing
it yourself!

What sound wakes you up in the morning? In the country, you might wake up to the sound of a rooster's crow.

SING this morning song.

I'LL RISE WHEN THE ROOSTER CROWS

Appalachian Folk Song
As Sung by Uncle Dave Macon

I'll rise when the rooster crows.
I'll rise when the rooster crows.
I'm going down south where
    the sun shines hot,
Down where the sugarcane grows.

SAY this rooster call four times as others sing the song.

One,	two,	cock-a- doo- dle doo!

In music, a pattern that repeats over and over is called an **ostinato.**

"Biddy, Biddy" comes from the warm island of Jamaica. Some words in the song tell about a game. Some words are simply nonsense.

SAY the words in "Biddy, Biddy" as you pat with the beat. On which beats are there four sounds? What are the words on these beats?

Biddy, Biddy

Jamaican Game Song

Biddy, Biddy, hol' fas' los' my gold ring,
Carry me to London, come back again.
Biddy, Biddy, hol' fas' los' my gold ring,
Carry me to London, come back again.

Phrase Your Ideas

This American folk song tells about farm life. Farmers try to reuse the materials that their farms produce so that nothing is wasted.

READ "The Old Sow's Hide," a song from America's past, and find what this farmer reused.

The Old Sow's Hide

American Folk Song

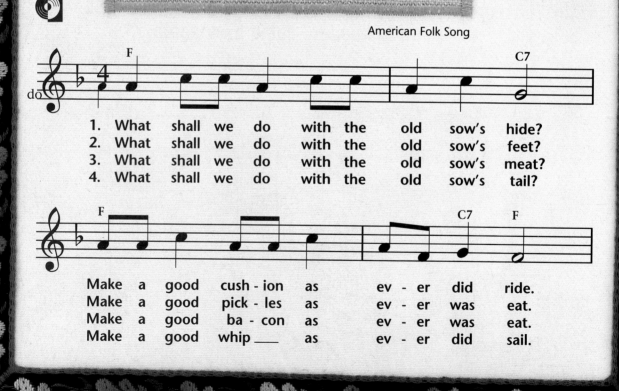

1. What shall we do with the old sow's hide?
2. What shall we do with the old sow's feet?
3. What shall we do with the old sow's meat?
4. What shall we do with the old sow's tail?

Make a good cush-ion as ev-er did ride.
Make a good pick-les as ev-er was eat.
Make a good ba-con as ev-er was eat.
Make a good whip___ as ev-er did sail.

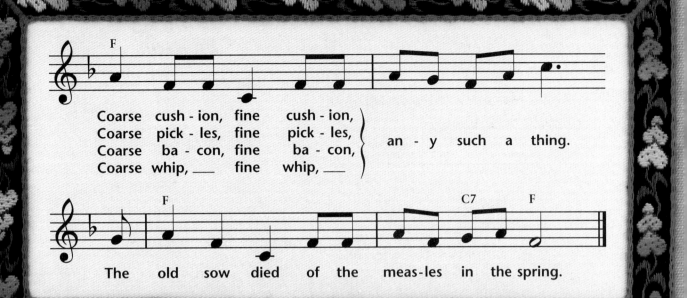

Coarse cush - ion, fine cush - ion,
Coarse pick - les, fine pick - les,
Coarse ba - con, fine ba - con,
Coarse whip, ___ fine whip, ___ an - y such a thing.

The old sow died of the meas-les in the spring.

When you create
a story, you put words and thoughts
into sentences. When you create music,
you put musical thoughts into musical sentences
called phrases. A **phrase** expresses a complete
musical idea. How many phrases are there in
"The Old Sow's Hide"?

In the movie *The Wizard of Oz,* a young girl named Dorothy finds herself in a strange land. Only a great wizard can help her get home to Kansas. This song is sung as she sets off to find the wizard.

The curved lines above the music show the phrases.

WE'RE OFF TO SEE THE WIZARD

Words by E.Y. Harburg
Music by Harold Arlen

Fol-low the yel-low brick road, __ Fol-low the yel-low brick road, __

Fol-low, fol-low, fol-low, fol-low, fol-low the yel-low brick road. __

Fol-low the rain-bow o-ver the stream, Fol-low the fel-low who fol-lows a dream.

Fol-low, fol-low, fol-low, fol-low, fol-low the yel-low brick road.

We're off to see the Wiz-ard, __ The won-der-ful Wiz-ard of Oz. __

IMAGINE you're on the yellow brick road as you trace the phrases in this song.

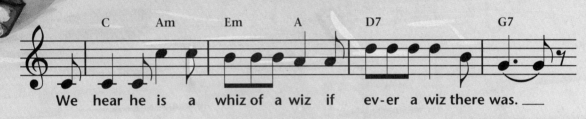

We hear he is a whiz of a wiz if ev-er a wiz there was. ___

If ev-er, oh, ev-er a wiz there was, The Wiz-ard of Oz is one be-coz,

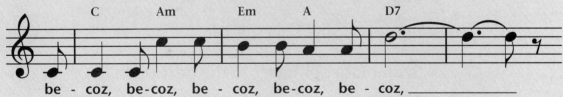

be - coz, be-coz, be - coz, be-coz, be - coz, _____

Be - coz of the won-der-ful things he does.

We're off to see the Wiz-ard, _ The won-der-ful Wiz-ard of Oz. ___

Notes that Step, Skip, and Repeat

When a melody moves, it can:

- **Step** higher or lower to the next pitch.
- **Skip** higher or lower over one or more pitches.
- **Repeat** on the same pitch.

The pitches in the melody of "Goin' to Ride Up in the Chariot" move by stepping, skipping, and repeating.

LISTEN to "Goin' to Ride Up in the Chariot" and find two wide skips.

Some people think of the chariot ride as a way of traveling to a better life.

Goin' to Ride Up in the Chariot

African American Spiritual

Goin' to ride up in the char - iot soon-er in the morn - ing.,

Soon-er in the morn-ing, Soon-er in the morn-ing. Ride up in the char-iot

Soon-er in the morn-ing, and I hope I'll join the band.

FISHING FOR SKIPS

This song is sometimes sung as people pull ropes and raise sails on fishing boats. The rhythm of the song helps them work together.

FIND the largest skip in this melody.

WANG Ü GER
CHINESE FISHING SONG

Chinese Folk Song
Collected and Transcribed
by Kathy B. Sorensen
English Version by MMH

Mandarin:	白	浪	滔	滔	我	不	怕
Pronunciation:	bɑi	lang	tau	tau	wɔ	bu	pɑ
English:	Though	the	waves ___	run ___	high	and	deep,

	掌	穩	舵	兒	往	前	划
	jang	wɛn	duɔ	ɚ	wang	chiɛn	hwɑ
	We	sail	on ___	the ___	course	we	keep.

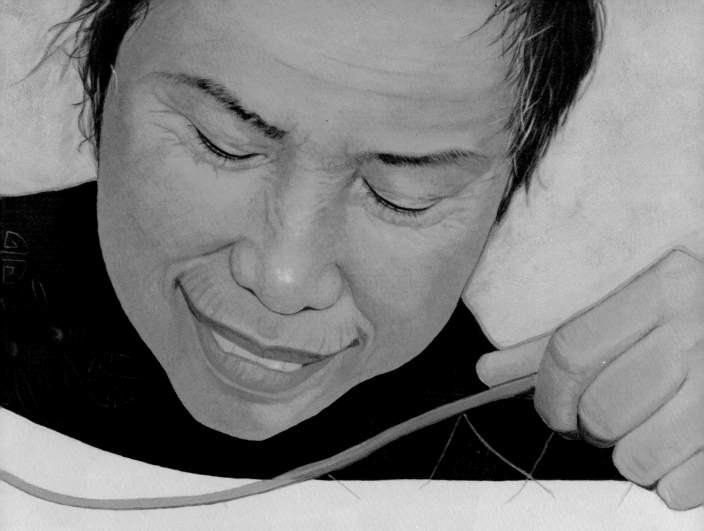

撒　網　　下　水　　　到　魚　家
sa　wang　　sia　shue　　　dau　yü　jia
Throw　the　　net ___ and ___　let　it　fall,

捕　條　　大　　魚　　笑　哈　　哈
bu　tiau　　da　　yü　　siau　ha　　ha
Catch　the　　big - gest ___　fish　of　all.

Four Sounds to a BEAT

COCKA

One part of the rooster's call, *cockadoodle,* has four sounds to a beat.

Cock- a-   doo- dle

In music, four sounds to a beat can look like this:

or this:

These are called **sixteenth notes.**

You can figure out a song you know from its rhythm.

CHOOSE a rhythm that matches the words *one, two, cockadoodle-doo!*

1.

2.

3.

4.

MATCH each word phrase to a rhythm above.

• *Rinktum body minchy cambo*
• *Biddy, Biddy, hol' fas' los' my gold ring*
• *Sooner in the morning, Sooner in the morning*

Overture to *The Marriage of Figaro*

by Wolfgang Amadeus Mozart

*The quick rhythms (♪♫♫), musical phrases, and tone
colors combine to make this music very exciting.*

LISTEN to this overture by Mozart. Stand when
you hear this pattern.

Wolfgang Amadeus

MOZART

Wolfgang Amadeus Mozart (1756–1791) was born in Austria. As a young child, he could play the piano perfectly. By the time he was five years old, he was already writing music. He and his sister traveled all over Europe performing for kings and queens. Mozart is considered one of the greatest musical geniuses who ever lived. However, during his lifetime, not everyone liked his music. Once, after hearing a piece by Mozart, a king said that Mozart wrote "too many notes." What do you think?

176

Mozart used many ♪♪♪♪ rhythms. This song, about a colorful market in Australia, also uses many ♪♪♪♪ rhythms. Every Saturday, people gather at Salamanca Market to shop for food and crafts.

READ the rhythms in "Salamanca Market."

Say *cockadoodle* for ♪♪♪♪ *rooster* for ♪ and *hen* for ♩

THINK IT THROUGH

Choose the name of a place. Sing "Salamanca Market" with the name you chose instead of the words *Salamanca Market*. Which way do you like the song better? Why?

do SING IT HIGH

You can learn to read songs with *do* in many different places.

Find *do* on this staff. It's on a ledger line.

do   re   mi   so   la

SING the first phrase of "I'll Rise When the Rooster Crows" using pitch syllables.

do	mi	so	so	so	mi	so
I'll	rise	when	the	roost	- er	crows.

SING the second phrase using pitch syllables and hum when you see "?"

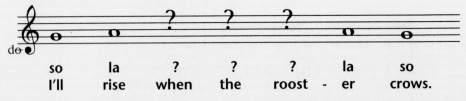

so	la	?	?	?	la	so
I'll	rise	when	the	roost	- er	crows.

Are the "?" pitches higher or lower than *la*?

This highest pitch is called *high do* or *do¹*.

Listen to the song and stand when you hear *do¹*.

178

SING IT LOW

I'll Rise When the Rooster Crows

Appalachian
Folk Song
As Sung by
Uncle Dave Macon

Even though *do* can be in different places on the staff, the pattern of pitches will always match the pattern on the pitch stairs.

FIND *do'* on the pitch stairs.

Use the pitch stairs to name the pitches in this song.

You can read all of the rhythms and pitches–including high *do*–in this marketplace song.

FIND each high *do* in the melody of "Salamanca Market."

SALAMANCA MARKET

Words and Music
by Mary Goetze

do

I must go to Sal - a - man - ca Mar - ket,

do

I must go to

Sal - a - man - ca Mar - ket in the morn - ing.

Sal - a - man - ca Mar - ket, Sal - a - man - ca Mar - ket in the

There's no place like Sal - a - man - ca Mar - ket, morn - ing. There's no place like Sal - a-man-ca Mar-ket all the day. Sal - a-man-ca Mar - ket, Sal - a-man-ca Mar-ket all the day.

A song that can be sung by two or more groups, each starting at different times, is called a **canon.**

SING **"Salamanca Market"** as a canon.

The melody of "Wang Ü Ger" has small and large skips. Where is the largest skip?

READ the first two lines of this song with pitch syllables.

Though the waves __ run __ high and deep,

We sail on __ the __ course we keep.

Throw the net __ and __ let it fall,

Catch the big - gest __ fish of all.

MELODY!

FIND the "?" on the pitch stairs.
What is the name of the new pitch?

Use the pitch stairs to
name the pitches used
in "Wang Ü Ger."

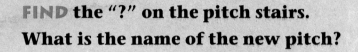

?'

do'

la

so

mi

re

do

183

Songs that use *do re mi so* and *la* have a special name.
The name uses the word *penta,* which is Greek for "five."

Make new words using the prefix "penta," or
create something imaginary.

unicorn

pentacorn

"Wang Ü Ger" has five pitches, so you can call this song **pentatonic.**

> –*penta* (meaning five)
> –*tonic* (meaning pitch)

Why is "Salamanca Market" a pentatonic song?

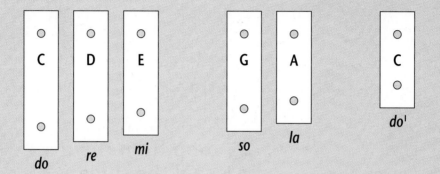

C do
D re
E mi
G so
A la
C do'

A **scale** is a group of pitches in order from lowest to highest.

SING the pitch syllables used in "Salamanca Market" in order from lowest to highest.

You just sang a **pentatonic scale!**

PLAY this scale before you sing "Salamanca Market."

do re mi   so la do'   la so mi re   do

MUSICAL CONVERSATIONS

READ this poem to find out how
the animals answer the questions.

The Secret Song

Who saw the petals
   drop from the rose?
I, said the spider,
But nobody knows.

Who saw the sunset
   flash on a bird?
I, said the fish,
But nobody heard.

Who saw the fog
   come over the sea?
I, said the sea pigeon,
Only me.

Who saw the first
   green light of the sun?
I, said the night owl,
The only one.

Who saw the moss
   creep over the stone?
I, said the grey fox,
All alone.

— *Margaret Wise Brown*

In music, some phrases are like questions, and some are like answers.

CLAP this musical question, and pat this musical answer.

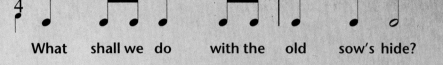

What   shall we   do   with the   old   sow's hide?

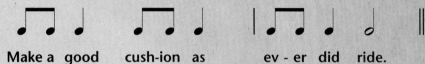

Make a   good   cush-ion   as   ev - er   did   ride.

Try clapping this question and answer with a friend.

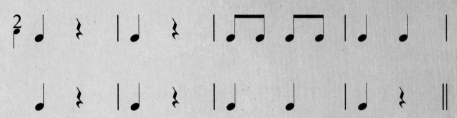

How are the phrases alike?

How are they different?

CLAP this question.

CREATE an answer by doing one of the following:

- Move the sixteenth notes to a new place.
- Add a rest for one or more beats.
- Make up a new rhythm for the last four beats.

Music played before a song starts is called an **introduction.** Music added to the end of a song is called a **coda.** The Italian word *coda* means "tail."

PERFORM the questions and answers you just created as an introduction and coda for "Biddy, Biddy."

BiDDY, BiDDY

Jamaican Game Song

Bid - dy, Bid - dy, hol' fas' los' my gold ring,

Car - ry me to Lon - don, come back a - gain.

Bid - dy, Bid - dy, hol' fas' los' my gold ring,

Car - ry me to Lon - don, come back a - gain.

FORM YOUR IDEAS

Just as you can combine sentences to make a paragraph, you can combine musical phrases to create a section of music. The three lines below make up the first section of "Goin' to Ride Up in the Chariot."

Goin' to Ride Up in the Chariot

African American Spiritual

A C   F   C

Goin' to ride up in the char - iot soon-er in the morn-ing,

C   F   C

Soon-er in the morn-ing, Soon-er in the morn-ing. Ride up in the char-iot

F   C   G7   C

Soon-er in the morn-ing, and I hope I'll join the band.

You can put sections of music together to create a longer song. Add this section to "Goin' to Ride Up in the Chariot."

B C   F   C   F   G7

Oh, Lord, have _ mer-cy on me,   Oh, Lord, have _ mer-cy on me,

C   F   C   G7   C

Oh, Lord, have _ mer-cy on me, and I hope I'll join the band.

Now the song has two sections. Label these sections with the letters *A* and *B.*

SING the song in this order: first section, second section, first section. How would you use the letters *A* and *B* to label this form?

DESIGN IN MUSIC: MEET THE RONDO!

Sections of music can be combined to make a long piece of music. A **rondo** is a long piece of music in which one section always returns. The sections in between are different.

LABEL these instruments with the letters *A, B,* and *C.*

vihuela

guitarrón

guitar

Each section of "Los mariachis" has a different melody and a different dance step.

LISTEN **to "Los mariachis" and pat with the beat each time you hear the A section.**

Los mariachis   Mexican Folk Music

"Los mariachis" is performed by a mariachi band. Which instrument plays the melody in the A section?

violin

trumpets

WORDS FOR THE WIZARD

Pretend you are lost in the land of Oz. The Wizard will grant your wish to go home if you can match these word phrases to the pictures.

- Rinktum body minchy cambo
- Make a good cushion
- Follow, follow, follow, follow,
- rise when the rooster crows
- There's no place like

CHECK IT OUT

1. On which beat do you hear four sixteenth notes?

   a. one **b.** two **c.** one **d.** two

2. Choose the rhythm you hear.

3. How many phrases do you hear?

   a. two **b.** three **c.** four **d.** more than four

4. Which pitches do you hear?

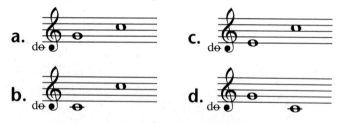

5. Choose the example you hear.

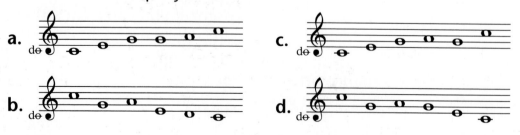

CREATE

Write a Musical Background

CREATE an eight-beat rhythm pattern. Draw these lines on a piece of paper.

Write one of these on each line.

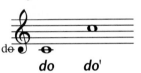

With a partner, put your rhythms together to make a sixteen-beat rhythm pattern. Decide how to play your rhythm on the two bells *do* (C) and *do'* (C').

PLAY your piece while someone else sings one of these songs.

- "The Old Sow's Hide"
- "Salamanca Market"
- "I'll Rise When the Rooster Crows"

Write

Pretend you are lost in the land of Oz. Write a letter to the Wizard explaining why you want to go home.

KASILYIO
The Wet Sage

Luiseño Lullaby

| Luiseño: | Ka | sil | yi | o ____ | pe | ne | wi | ke | pe | ne | wi | ke | eu |
| Pronunciation: | kɑ | sɪl | yɪ | o | pɛ | nɛ | wɪ | kɛ | pɛ | nɛ | wɪ | kɛ | ɛu |

| Ka | sil | yi | o ____ | pe | ne | wi | ke | pe | ne | wi | ke | eu | eu | eu |
| kɑ | sɪl | yɪ | o | pɛ | nɛ | wɪ | kɛ | pɛ | nɛ | wɪ | kɛ | ɛu | ɛu | ɛu |

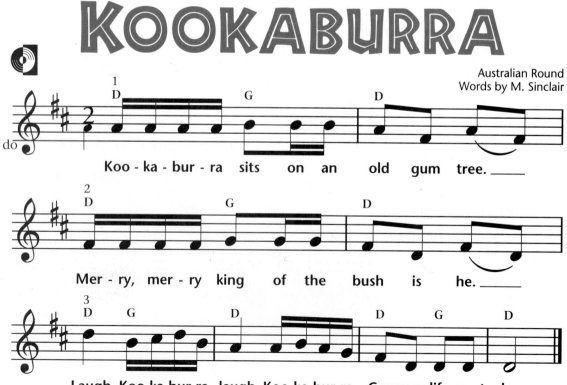

KOOKABURRA

Australian Round
Words by M. Sinclair

Koo - ka - bur - ra sits on an old gum tree. ____

Mer - ry, mer - ry king of the bush is he. ____

Laugh, Koo - ka - bur-ra, laugh, Koo-ka-bur-ra, Gay your life must be.

198

The Old Brass Wagon

Midwestern American Singing Game

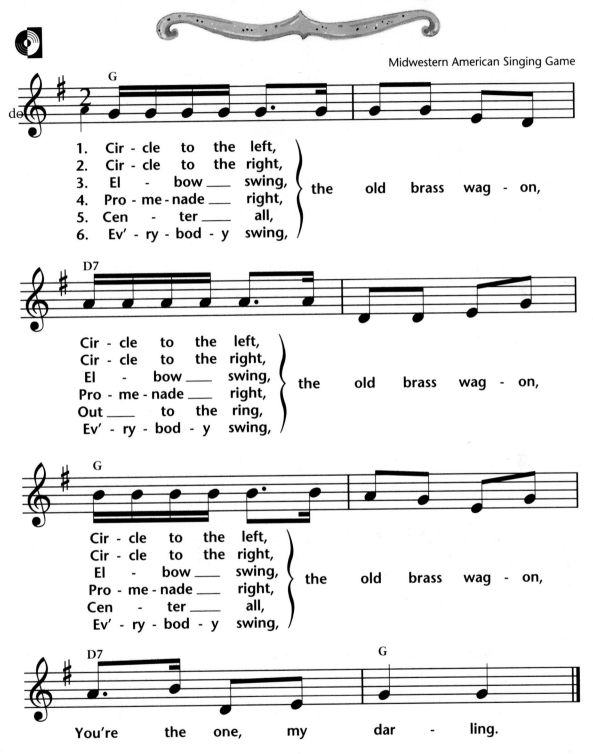

1. Cir - cle   to   the   left,
2. Cir - cle   to   the   right,
3. El -   bow ___ swing,   } the   old   brass   wag - on,
4. Pro - me - nade ___ right,
5. Cen - ter ___   all,
6. Ev' - ry - bod - y   swing,

Cir - cle   to   the   left,
Cir - cle   to   the   right,
El -   bow ___ swing,   } the   old   brass   wag - on,
Pro - me - nade ___ right,
Out ___   to   the   ring,
Ev' - ry - bod - y   swing,

Cir - cle   to   the   left,
Cir - cle   to   the   right,
El -   bow ___ swing,   } the   old   brass   wag - on,
Pro - me - nade ___ right,
Cen - ter ___   all,
Ev' - ry - bod - y   swing,

You're   the   one,   my   dar - ling.

THE FOX

English Folk Song

Freely

F

1. The   fox   went   out   on   a   chill - y   night,
2. He   ran   till he   came   to   a   great   big   bin,
3. He   grabbed the   gray   goose ___   by   the   neck;
4. Then   old   Mo-ther Flip-per-Flop - per   jumped out of   bed.
5. Then   John   he   went   to   the   top   of the   hill;

F   C7

He   prayed   for   the   moon   for   to   give   him   light,
Where the   ducks   and   the   geese   were ___   put   there - in.
Threw   a ___   duck   a -   cross   his   back.
Out   of   the   win - dow   she   cocked   her   head,
Blew   his ___   horn   both ___   loud   and   shrill;

F

For   he'd   man - y   a   mile   to
"A ___   cou - ple   of   you   will
He ___   did - n't   mind   their
Cry - ing,   "John, ___   John!   The
The ___   fox ___   he   said,   "I'd   bet - ter

B♭   F   C7

go   that   night   a - fore   he   reached the
grease   my   chin   a - fore   I   leave   this
quack,   quack,   quack   And their   legs   all   dang - ling
gray   goose is   gone   And   the   fox   is   on   the
flee   with my   kill   Or   they'll   soon   be   on   my

200

town - o,   town - o,   town - o,   He'd
town - o,   town - o,   town - o,   A
down - o,   down - o,   down - o,   He
town - o,   town - o,   town - o!"   Cry-ing,
trail - o,   trail - o,   trail - o!"   The

man - y   a   mile   to   go   that   night
cou - ple   of   you   will   grease   my   chin
did - n't   mind   their   quack,   quack,   quack
"John, _____ John!   The   gray   goose is   gone
fox ____ he   said,   "I'd   bet - ter   flee   with my   kill

A - fore he reached the   town - o. _____
A - fore I leave this   town - o." _____
And their legs all dang - ling down - o. _____
And the fox is on   the   town - o!" _____
Or they'll soon be on   my   trail - o!" _____

6. He ran till he came to his cozy den,
   There were the little ones, eight, nine, ten.
   They said, "Daddy, better go back again
   'Cause it must be a mighty fine town-o, town-o, town-o!"
   They said, "Daddy, . . ."

7. Then the fox and his wife without any strife,
   Cut up the goose with a fork and knife;
   They never had such a supper in their life
   And the little ones chewed on the bones-o, bones-o, bones-o.
   They never had . . .

ENCORE

FIT AS A FIDDLE

The fiddle was one of the most popular instruments in colonial America. It was easy to carry and was made by hand. Colonists enjoyed playing songs and dances on the fiddle.

LISTENING

Doubtful Shepherd *English Dance Tune*

An evening gathering of friends in colonial times often ended with dancing. "Doubtful Shepherd" is a short dance that the New England colonists enjoyed.

LISTEN to the sound of the fiddle in this music.

Try this dance yourself. Line up as shown in the picture. The arrows show you how to begin. First, girls hold hands and walk a pathway behind boys. Then, boys hold hands and walk behind girls.

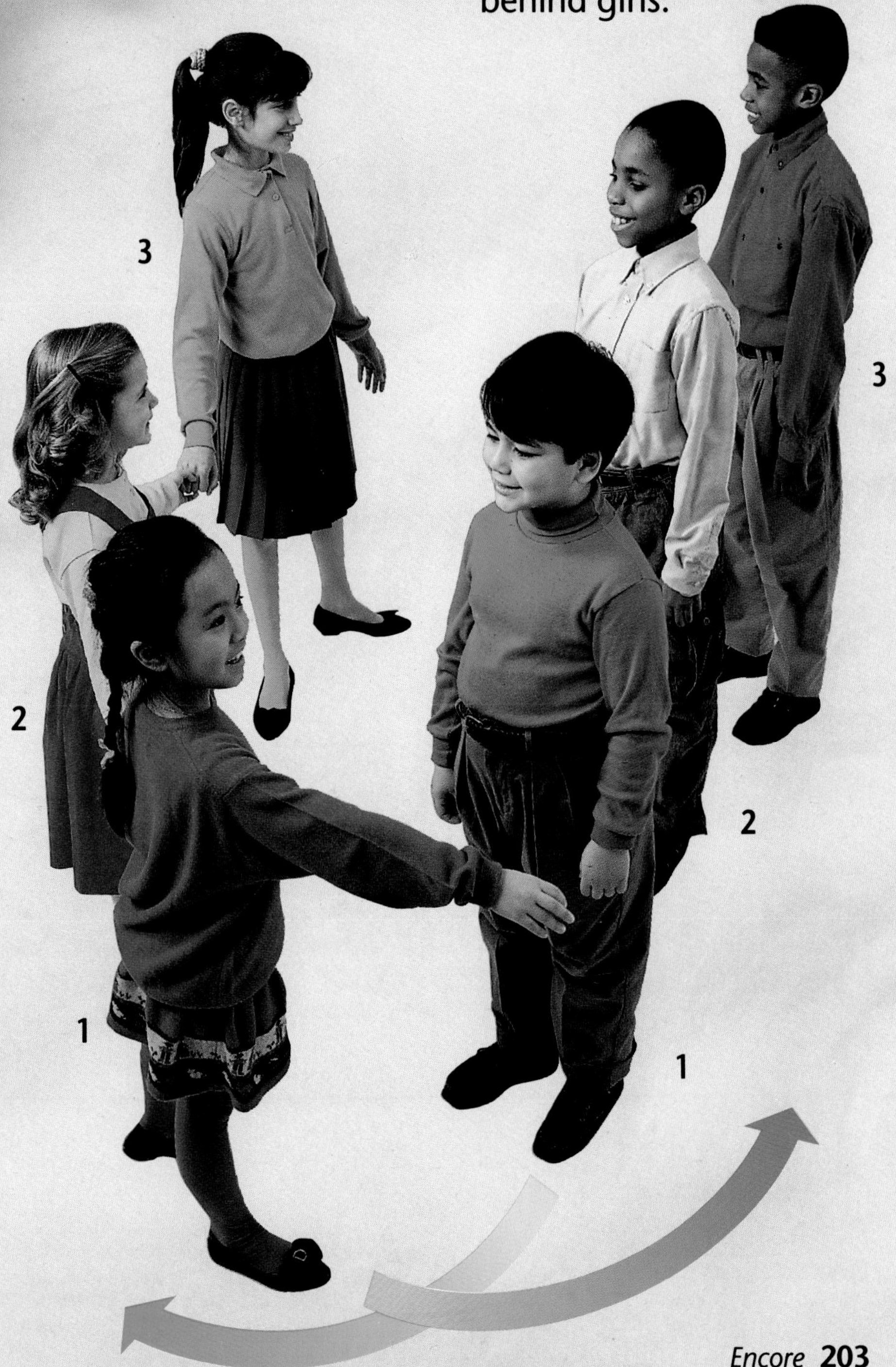

3

3

2

2

1

1

The fiddle is also called a violin. The violin was developed long ago in Italy. Violin makers such as Andrea Amati and Antonio Stradivari looked for ways to make the tone louder, clearer, and more beautiful.

The form of the violin has changed very little in 400 years. Violin makers still work very carefully to produce the most perfect violin possible. The right wood must be chosen and formed into parts of the instrument. Then these parts will be fitted together.

Violin music sounds very different from fiddle music. The beautiful sound of the violin makes it a very important part of the orchestra. It is the smallest and highest-sounding member of the string family, and often plays the melody.

LISTENING

Waltz Finale

from **The Nutcracker** *by Peter Tchaikovsky*

LISTEN to the "Waltz Finale." The violins are playing the melody.

Work, Play—

They Were My People

They were those who cut cane
to the rhythm of the sunbeat.

They were those who carried cane
to the rhythm of the sunbeat.

They were those who crushed cane
to the rhythm of the sunbeat.

They were women weeding, carrying babies
to the rhythm of the sunbeat.

They were my people working so hard
to the rhythm of the sunbeat.

They were my people, working so hard
to the rhythm of the sunbeat—long ago
to the rhythm of the sunbeat.

—Grace Nichols

Music can be a natural part of work. This song about working on a riverboat helps you to hear the "swoosh" of the paddle as it cuts through the water.

Words and Music
by Fran Smartt Andicott

1. Work - ing   on   the   Del - ta   Queen,
2. Old   deck   shoes   and   worn   blue   jeans.
3. Not   a   show   for the   sil - ver   screen.
4. You'll   be   glad   you   made   the   scene.

tough-est   job   you've   ev - er __ seen.   This old   riv - er's
Make   a   meal   of   pork __ and __ beans.   Riv - er   boat stands
Boat's new pas-sen-gers   turn - in' __ green.   This old   riv - er's a
I've   been here   since I   turned _ eight - een.   Want to   see   a

brown and green;   Trick - y   cur - rents   make her mean. __
tall   and lean,   Keep her decks all   spot-less clean. __
tough ma - rine.   For   teach-ing   les - sons,   she's the dean. __
real   ma-chine?   Come and   ride   the   Del - ta Queen! __

B

Swing

1.–3.   Won't you come a-long with me   (ch   ch ___)

might-y Mis-sis-sip-pi   (ch   ch ___) {
will   give us a   ride. __
is   a   sight to _   see. __
keeps   flow-in' _   south. __
}

Go back to the beginning and sing to the end
(Da Capo al Fine)

(ch ch ___) She's got old   St. Lou-is right at her   side. _____
(ch ch ___)   Rock-in'and rol-lin' past Mem-phis, Ten - nes - see.
(ch ch ___) She's got New   Or-leans' _ foot in her   mouth. _____

SONGS FOR WORK

People everywhere create songs for working and playing. This game song comes from the Maori people in New Zealand. In the Maori language, *tititorea* means "little sticks." Some Maori people sing this song as they play a game with the sticks.

LISTEN to "Tititorea" as you perform this movement. Say "Floor, tap, out."

1. Tap floor.

AND PLAY

3. Move sticks apart.

2. Tap sticks together.

The beats in "Tititorea" are grouped in sets of three. The first beat in each set is the strong beat, or downbeat. Try a different movement to show the strong beats.

LISTEN to "Tititorea" again and tap the floor on Beat 1. Freeze on Beats 2 and 3.

Workers sing "One, Two, Three!" as they work in the cane fields in Barbados.

CREATE a four-beat movement ostinato for "One, Two, Three!" Use a heavier movement on the downbeat.

One, Two, Three!

Words and Music
by Maurice Gardner
In the style of a Barbados Work Song

1.–4. One, two, three!

C

Cut down de sug - ar cane all day.
Bun - dle de sug - ar cane all day.
Load up de sug - ar truck all day.
Walk down de mar - ket road all day.

C7   F

One, two, three!

Cut down de sug - ar cane all day.
Bun - dle de sug - ar cane all day.
Load up de sug - ar truck all day.
Walk down de mar - ket road all day.

F   Gm

One, two, three!

Cut down de sug - ar cane all day.
Bun - dle de sug - ar cane all day.
Load up de sug - ar truck all day.
Walk down de mar - ket road all day.

Work all de day-o, work all de day-o,

Cut down de sug-ar cane all day.
Bun-dle de sug-ar cane all day.
Load up de sug-ar truck all day.
Walk down de mar-ket road all day.

Work all de day-o, work all de day-o,

cut down de sug-ar cane.
bun-dle de sug-ar cane.
load up de sug-ar truck.
walk down de mar-ket road.

LISTENING

Cuequita de los Coyas

Andean Highlands Folk Music

The Coyas people come from the Andes Mountains in South America. They dance to this colorful native flute music. Cuequita de los Coyas *means "Dance of the Coyas."*

CHOOSE the beat grouping that matches "Cuequita de los Coyas."

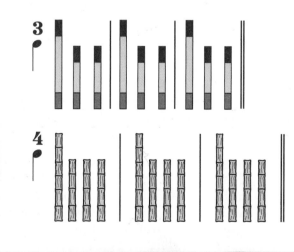

AN UPBEAT JOKE!

Do you think this is a song for work or a song for play? Why?

There's a Hole in the Bucket

American Dialogue Song
Traditional German Melody "Liebe Heinrich"

1. There's a hole in the buck-et, dear Li-za, dear Li-za,
2. Mend the hole, then, dear Geor-gie, dear Geor-gie, dear Geor-gie,
3. With ___ what shall I mend it, dear Li-za, dear Li-za,
4. With a straw, ___ dear Geor-gie, dear Geor-gie, dear Geor-gie,
5. The ___ straw is too long, ___ dear Li-za, dear Li-za,

There's a hole in the buck-et, dear Li-za, a hole.
Mend the hole, then, dear Geor-gie, dear Geor-gie, the hole.
With ___ what shall I mend it, dear Li-za, with what?
With a straw, ___ dear Geor-gie, dear Geor-gie, a straw.
The ___ straw is too long, ___ dear Li-za, too long.

6. Cut the straw, dear Georgie,
   dear Georgie, dear Georgie,
   Cut the straw, dear Georgie,
   dear Georgie, the straw.

7. With what shall I cut it,
   dear Liza, . . . with what?

8. With a knife, dear Georgie,
   . . . a knife.

9. The knife is too dull,
   dear Liza, . . . too dull.

10. Then sharpen it, dear Georgie,
    . . . then sharpen it.

11. With what shall I sharpen it,
    dear Liza, . . . with what?

12. With a stone, dear Georgie,
    . . . a stone.

13. The stone is too dry,
    dear Liza, . . . too dry.

14. Then wet it, dear Georgie,
    . . . then wet it.

15. With what shall I wet it,
    dear Liza, . . . with what?

16. With water, dear Georgie,
    . . . with water.

17. In what shall I get it,
    dear Liza, . . . in what?

18. In a bucket, dear Georgie,
    . . . in a bucket.

19. There's a hole in the bucket,
    dear Liza, . . . a hole.

How many phrases are in each verse?

AN UPBEAT PHRASE!

PAT, clap, and snap as you sing "There's a Hole in the Bucket."

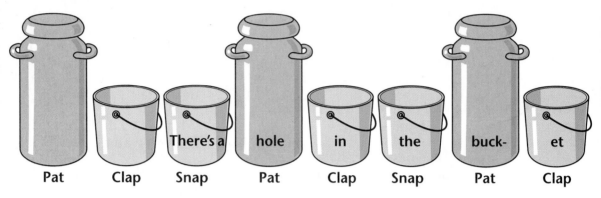

There's a	hole	in	the	buck-	et
Pat	Clap	Snap	Pat	Clap	Snap	Pat	Clap

Do the phrases begin on Beat 1, 2, or 3?

When a phrase starts before the first downbeat, it starts on an upbeat.

This Creole lullaby is from Louisiana.
The Creole culture is a mix of French,
Spanish, and African traditions.

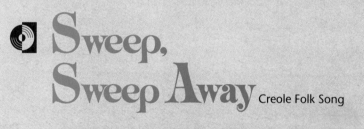

Sweep, Sweep Away
Creole Folk Song

Sweep, sweep, sweep away,

Sweep the road of dreams,

People say that, in the night,

The turtle will talk, it seems.

The turtle will talk, it seems.

Which phrases begin on Beat 1, the
downbeat? The upbeat?

Singing with Added Sounds

A lullaby like "Sweep, Sweep Away" is usually sung by one person, without any other musical sounds. Some songs are sung with **accompaniment,** or other musical sounds added to them.

LISTEN to the accompaniment in "Sandy Land."

No Accompaniment

Accompaniment

You can add your own accompaniment to "Sandy Land."

SING "Sandy Land," snapping on the words in blue and patting on the words in red.

Sandy Land Texas Folk Song

1. I make my living in the sandy land,
   I make my living in the sandy land,
   I make my living in the sandy land,
   Oh ladies, fare you well.

2. They raise big taters in the sandy land,
   They raise big taters in the sandy land,
   They raise big taters in the sandy land,
   Oh ladies, fare you well.

3. Sift the meal and save the bran,
   Sift the meal and save the bran,
   Sift the meal and save the bran,
   Oh ladies, fare you well.

4. One more river I'm bound to cross,
   One more river I'm bound to cross,
   One more river I'm bound to cross,
   Oh ladies, fare you well.

LISTEN to "Sandy Land" and move with a friend when you hear the accompaniment. Freeze when you hear only singing.

The guitar is used by many people to accompany songs. Why do you think the guitar is so popular?

meet Sally Rogers

Sally Rogers is a strong believer in saving our planet and creating world peace. She writes many songs with these themes. If you went to one of her concerts, you'd hear her clear soprano voice and see her play stringed instruments, including a guitar, banjo, and an Appalachian dulcimer. In her warm and friendly way, she'd invite you to sing along!

THINK IT THROUGH

What other musical instruments could you play to accompany "Sandy Land"? Why would these instruments make a good accompaniment?

ACCOMPANIMENT WITH CHORDS

Some accompaniments are made up of chords. A **chord** is made when three or more pitches are sounded together. Instruments such as guitars, pianos, autoharps, or bells can produce chords. Line up the bells like the pictures below and take turns playing these chords.

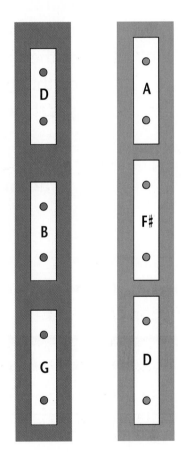

CHOOSE one bell from either the red set or the blue set. Play the bell as you sing the song on page 219.

You can also make a chord with voices. How could singers make a chord?

Notes that Last

The words in "Tititorea" tell an old Polynesian story. They tell how sad *Rangi,* the sky, is to be apart from *Papa,* the earth. The Maori people sing this song as they perform the stick game.

PLAY the Maori stick game on page 210 to accompany "Tititorea."

TITITOREA
MAORI STICK GAME

New Zealand Folk Song
Collected and Transcribed
by Kathy B. Sorensen

Maori: E hi - ne ho - ki mai ra.
Pronunciation: e hi ne ho ki mai ra

E pa - pa___ wai - a - ri ta - ku nei___ ma - hi,
e pa pa wai a ri ta ku nei ma hi

ta - ku nei___ ma - hi tu - ku roi - ma ta. Au
ta ku neɪ ma hi tu ku rɔɪ ma ta au

e au - e___ ka - ma - te au,
e au e ka ma te au

Go back to the beginning and sing to the end
(Da Capo al Fine)

E hi - ne ho - ki mai ra.
e hi ne ho ki maɪ ɾa

DOTTED HALF NOTES

What does the meter sign $\frac{3}{4}$ tell you?

Find the 𝅗𝅥. in "Tititorea." Then tap on the symbols below as you listen to "Tititorea."

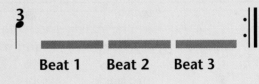

Beat 1   Beat 2   Beat 3

Trace the line when you hear a 𝅗𝅥.

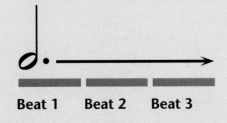

Beat 1   Beat 2   Beat 3

A **dotted half note** (𝅗𝅥.) lasts three beats. How many dotted half notes are in "Tititorea"?

When you watch a sunset, you can have many different feelings. What words in the first verse of this song tell you how this person is feeling?

EVERY NIGHT

Appalachian Folk Song

do

1. Ev' - ry   night   when the sun goes ___ in,
(2.) love don't weep,   true ___ love don't ___ mourn.
(3.) wish to the Lord,   that ___ train would ___ come.

      ev' - ry   night   when the sun goes   in,
True love don't weep,   true ___ love don't mourn.
   I wish to the Lord,   that ___ train would come.

      ev' - ry   night   when the sun goes ___ in,
True love don't weep,   true ___ love don't ___ mourn.
   I wish to the Lord,   that ___ train would ___ come.

   I hang down my head   and mourn-ful ___ cry.   2. True
I'm go - ing   a - way   to Mar - ble ___ Town.   3. I
And take ____ me back   where I come ___ from.

In ⁴/₄ meter, a sound that lasts a whole measure, or four beats, is called a **whole note.** A silence that lasts a whole measure is called a **whole rest** (–).

TAP this ostinato as you listen to "Every Night."

"Sweep, Sweep Away" is also in $\frac{4}{4}$ meter. It has four beats in each measure.

FIND the whole note (o) in "Sweep, Sweep Away."
Now find the dotted half notes (𝅗𝅥.).

Sweep, Sweep Away

Creole Folk Song

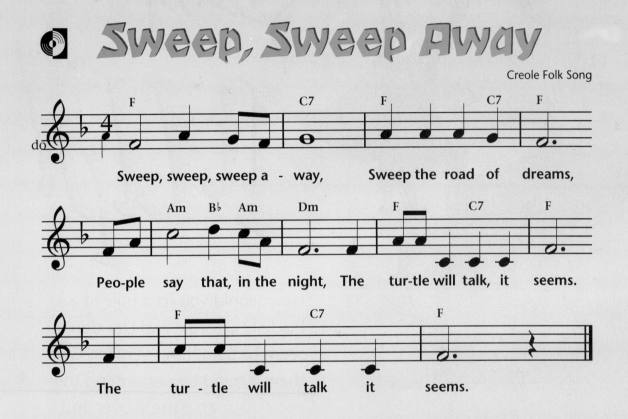

Sweep, sweep, sweep a - way, Sweep the road of dreams,

Peo-ple say that, in the night, The tur-tle will talk, it seems.

The tur - tle will talk it seems.

SING "Sweep, Sweep Away" as you watch the notation. Tap four times when you sing a whole note (o). Tap three times when you sing a dotted half note (𝅗𝅥.).

Snap It Up!

How would you fix a hole in a bucket? Georgie and Liza don't seem to be getting very far. Give them a hand by performing the pat-clap-snap pattern over and over as you sing this song. Start by snapping on the upbeat *There's a . . .*

There's a Hole in the Bucket

American Dialogue Song
Traditional German Melody "Liebe Heinrich"

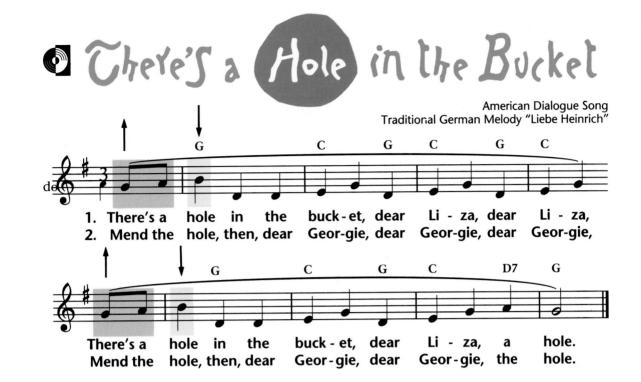

1. There's a hole in the buck-et, dear Li-za, dear Li-za,
2. Mend the hole, then, dear Geor-gie, dear Geor-gie, dear Geor-gie,

There's a hole in the buck-et, dear Li-za, a hole.
Mend the hole, then, dear Geor-gie, dear Geor-gie, the hole.

The arrows show the upbeats and downbeats.

SING these two verses again. Snap-pat only on the arrows.

"There's a Hole in the Bucket" is in $\frac{3}{4}$ meter, but the last measure has only 2 beats. Where's the third beat?

HINT: Perform the song twice, using the pat-clap-snap pattern.

LISTEN to "Ton moulin" for the rhythm of the repeating words.

Ton moulin
Your Windmill

French Folk Song
English Version by MMH

French: Ton mou - lin, ton mou - lin, ton mou - lin va trop vi - te,
Pronunciation: tɔ̃ mu lɛ̃ tɔ̃ mu lɛ̃ tɔ̃ mu lɛ̃ va tɾo vi tə
English: Ton mou - lin, ton mou - lin, your __ mill turns too quick-ly.

Ton mou - lin, ton mou - lin, ton mou - lin va trop fort!
tɔ̃ mu lɛ̃ tɔ̃ mu lɛ̃ tɔ̃ mu lɛ̃ va tɾo fɔɾ
Ton mou - lin, ton mou - lin, your __ mill turns too strong!

Ton mou - lin, ton mou - lin va trop vi - te,
tɔ̃ mu lɛ̃ tɔ̃ mu lɛ̃ va tɾo vi tə
Ton mou - lin, ton mou - lin turns too quick - ly,

Ton mou - lin, ton mou - lin va trop fort!
tɔ̃ mu lɛ̃ tɔ̃ mu lɛ̃ va tɾo fɔɾ
Ton mou - lin, ton mou - lin turns too strong!

Ton mou - lin, ton mou - lin, ton mou - lin va trop vi - te,
tɔ̃ mu lɛ̃ tɔ̃ mu lɛ̃ tɔ̃ mu lɛ̃ va tro vi tə
Ton mou - lin, ton mou - lin, your __ mill turns too quick-ly.

Ton mou - lin, ton mou - lin, ton mou - lin va trop fort!
tɔ̃ mu lɛ̃ tɔ̃ mu lɛ̃ tɔ̃ mu lɛ̃ va tro fɔr
Ton mou - lin, ton mou - lin, your __ mill turns too strong!

Which section of "Ton moulin" begins
on an upbeat? Downbeat?

PERFORM a dance with each section
of "Ton moulin." Do a millwheel
movement for section A. Choose your
partner and whirl on section B.

Meter Match

Do you ever make up rhymes when you walk to school or go for a long car ride? Maybe you sing songs or trade tongue twisters with a friend. Try this rhyme. Change *salt and PEPPER* to the silliest food you can think of!

Mabel, Mabel

Mabel, Mabel, set the table, Don't forget the salt and PEPPER!

—*Carl Withers*

CHOOSE one of these items and say the poem again.

- mustard
- lemonade
- spoons
- red hot pepper

Mabel's in such a hurry she can't decide
whether to say this poem in $\frac{4}{4}$ or $\frac{3}{4}$ meter!

SAY "Mabel, Mabel" in $\frac{4}{4}$ meter.

Ma - bel, Ma - bel, set the ta - ble. Don't for - get the _____ .

SAY "Mabel, Mabel" in $\frac{3}{4}$ meter.

Ma - bel, Ma - bel, set the ta - ble. Don't for - get the _____ .

Which do you like better? Why?

LISTENING

Allemande Tripla

by Johann Hermann Schein

Sometimes composers use both $\frac{3}{2}$ and $\frac{4}{2}$ when they write music. This music was written hundreds of years ago by a German composer named Johann Hermann Schein.

LISTEN to the sounds of recorders and lutes in this music.

THE CONCERT

This group of musicians was painted over 300 years ago by J. van Bijlert. How are these instruments similar to, or different from instruments you see or play today?

"Ton moulin" and "Allemande Tripla" have two things in common. They both change meters, and they both have A and B sections.

LISTENING MAP *Follow the listening map below to find an added section in "Allemande Tripla." What is the letter of this new section? Which sections are in $\frac{4}{?}$? In $\frac{3}{?}$?*

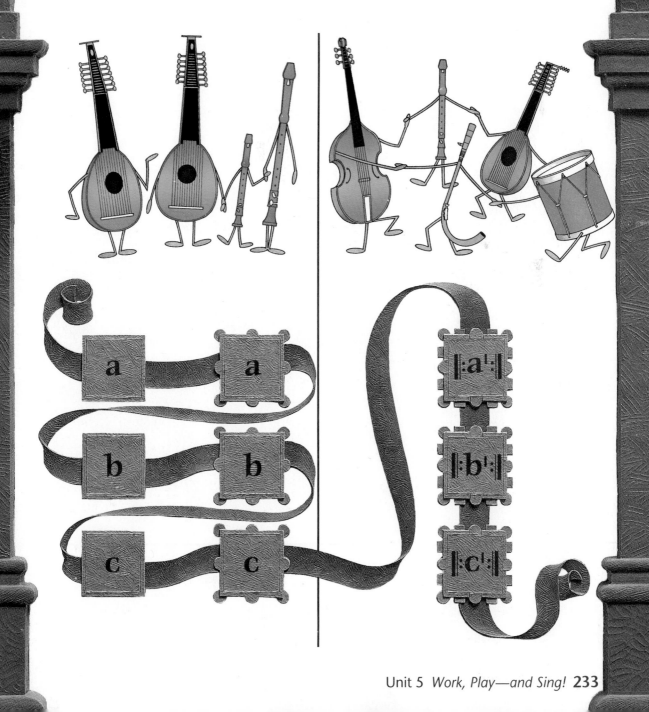

TRADITIONS IN SONG

If you go to the Cattaraugus reservation, in western New York state, you might see this Seneca Stomp Dance.

Senecas are a Native American nation. Senecas perform stomp-dance songs to start a ceremony or an evening of fun. Creek, Seminole, and Cherokee nations also perform stomp dances.

For hundreds of years, people have learned songs by listening to other people perform them. You can learn music this way, too!

LISTEN to "Seneca Stomp Dance" performed by the people of the Seneca nation.

Seneca Stomp Dance
by Avery Jimerson

Ya yo we ye ha, Yo we ya,
(repeat four times)

Ya yo we ye ha, Yo we ya,
We ha yo we ye ha, Yo we ya,
(repeat four times) Yo.

Did you hear a repeated pattern?

PERFORM the stomp-dance movement as you sing the song.

Slide your right foot forward, then "stomp" your left foot next to it.

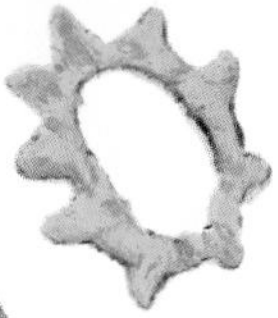

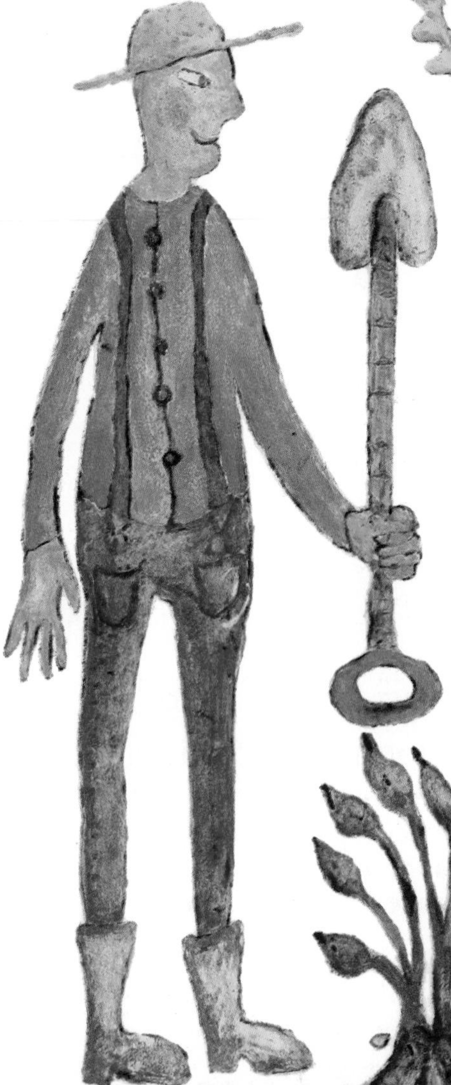

You can read pitches using pitch syllables. You can also read pitches using letter names. The **treble clef** or **G clef** (𝄞) at the beginning of a staff tells you that the pitch on the second line is G. What are the letter names of the next two pitches?

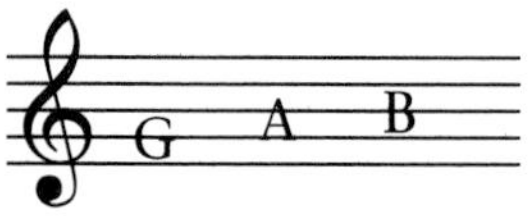

G A B

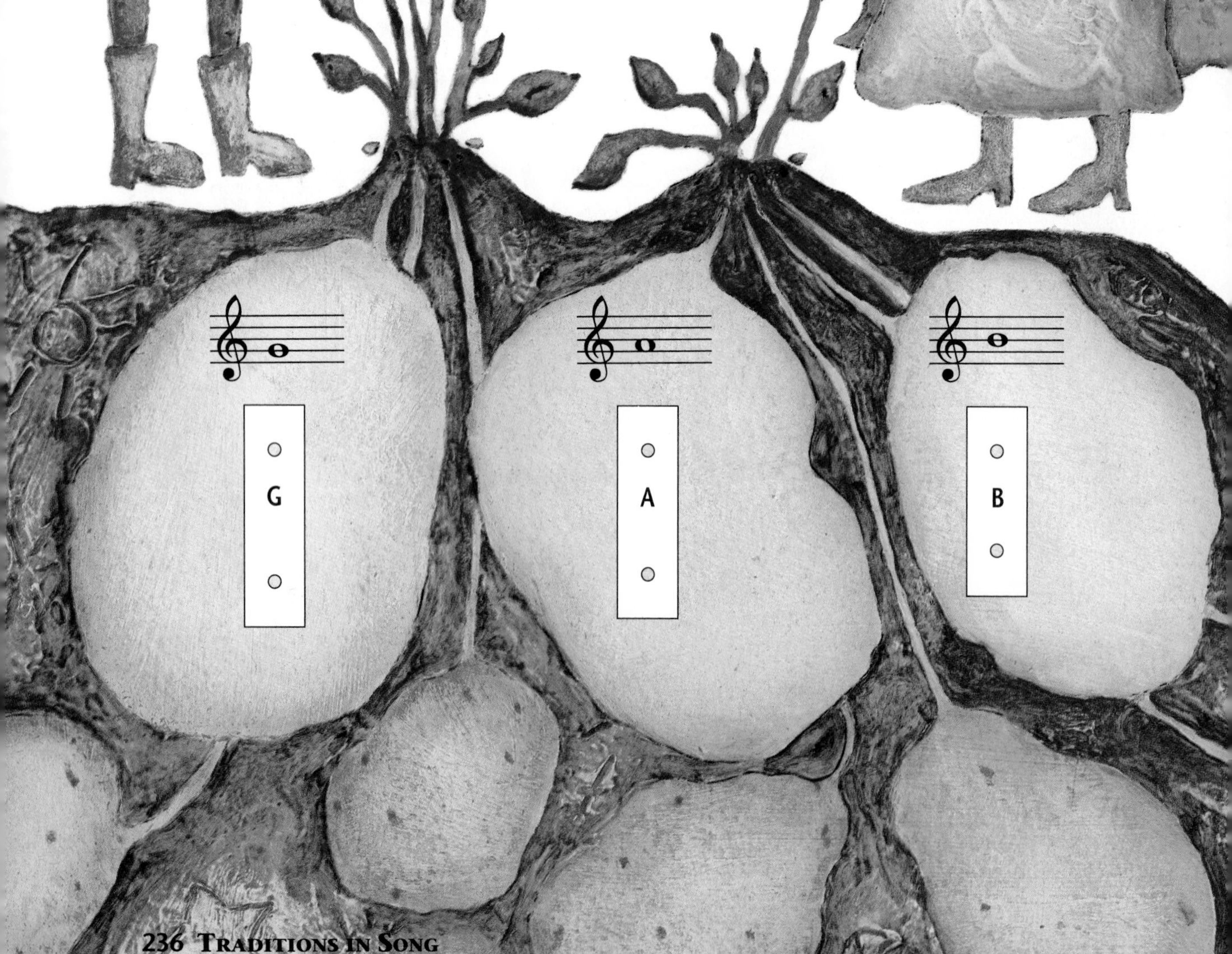

G

A

B

SING "Sandy Land" and play the
tinted pitches (G, A, and B) on bells.

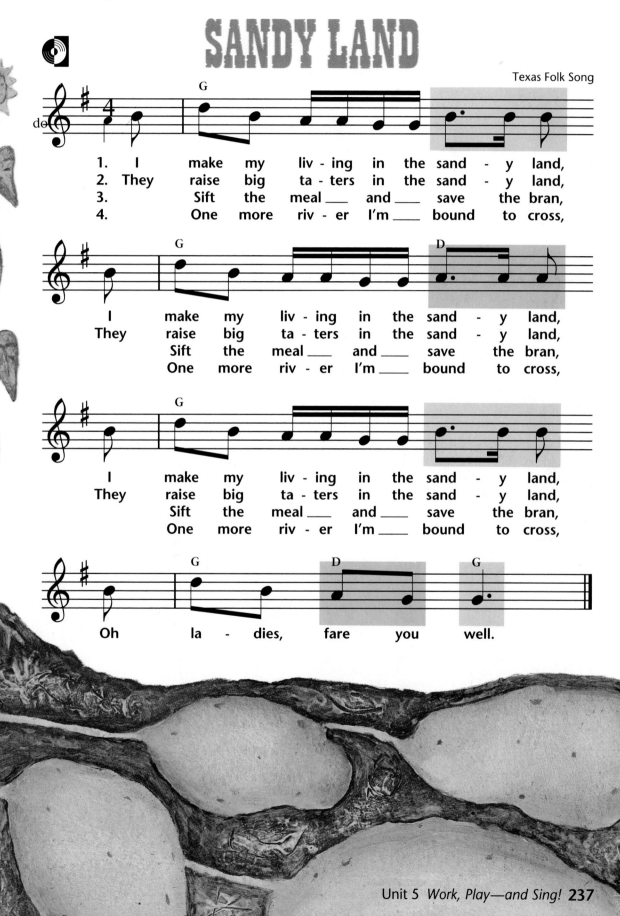

SANDY LAND

Texas Folk Song

1. I make my liv - ing in the sand - y land,
2. They raise big ta - ters in the sand - y land,
3. Sift the meal ___ and ___ save the bran,
4. One more riv - er I'm ___ bound to cross,

I make my liv - ing in the sand - y land,
They raise big ta - ters in the sand - y land,
Sift the meal ___ and ___ save the bran,
One more riv - er I'm ___ bound to cross,

I make my liv - ing in the sand - y land,
They raise big ta - ters in the sand - y land,
Sift the meal ___ and ___ save the bran,
One more riv - er I'm ___ bound to cross,

Oh la - dies, fare you well.

SHARP CONTRAS

THROUGH-GOING LINE

Wassily Kandinsky used loud colors and shapes with sharp edges to create *Through-going Line,* a painting that is full of explosive energy. What words would you use to describe this painting?

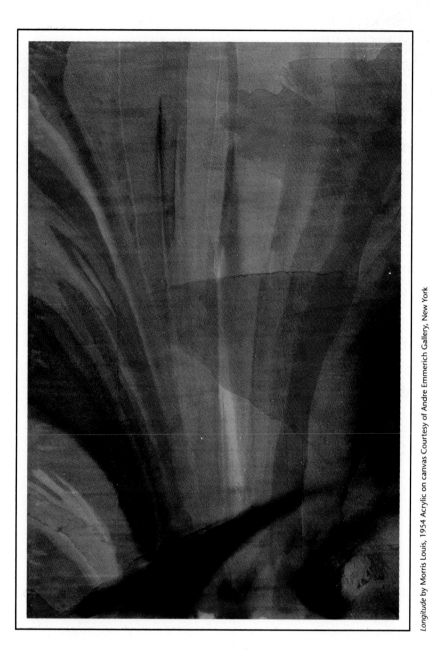

Longitude by Morris Louis, 1954 Acrylic on canvas Courtesy of Andre Emmerich Gallery, New York

LONGITUDE

Morris Louis used pastel colors and long lines to create *Longitude.* What words would you use to describe this painting?

SING "Every Night" and "One, Two, Three!" **Which painting best matches the feeling of each song? Why?**

Sometimes a song can have sections that feel very different. The song "Ton moulin" has a middle section that feels different from the first or last section.

PERFORM the movements shown on page 229. Then sing "Ton moulin" to find which section has a (𝅗𝅥.).

PLAY this melodic ostinato on bells during the A sections of "Ton moulin."

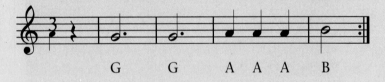

G   G   A A A   B

These instruments are used in
"Allemande Tripla."

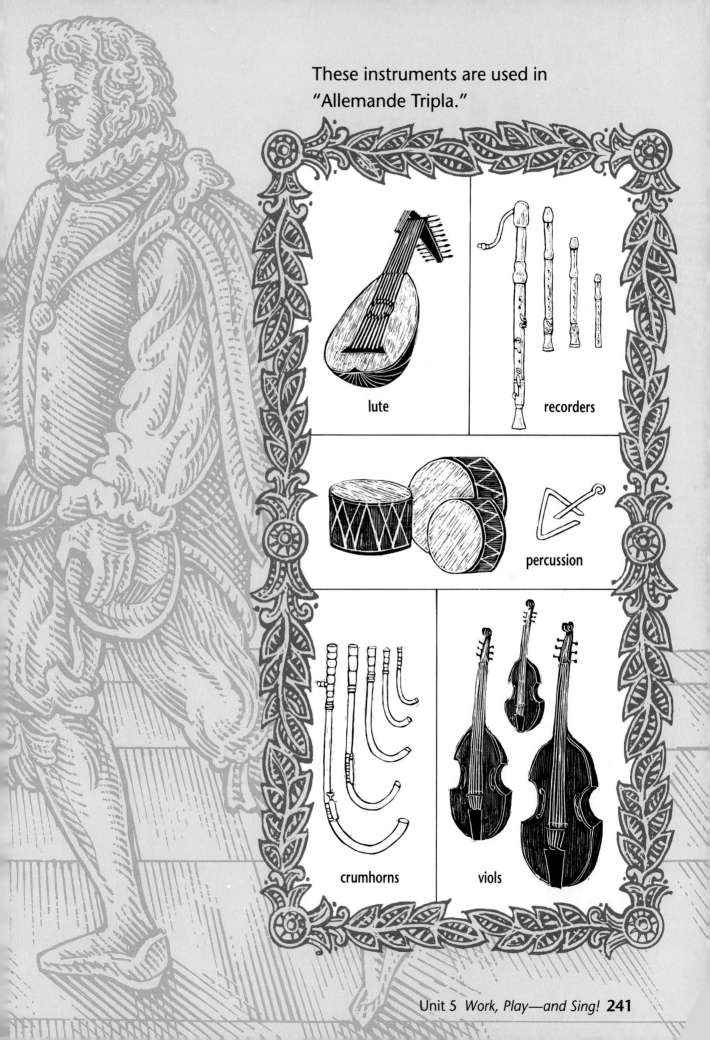

lute

recorders

percussion

crumhorns

viols

REVIEW

UPBEAT SONGS

Match each song title to a picture. Sing
each song and perform the movements.
Then decide whether the song is for work or play.

- "One, Two, Three"
- "Tititorea"
- "Sweep, Sweep Away"
- "There's a Hole in
  the Bucket"
- "Ton moulin"

Match one of these symbols to each song.

Then match one of these meter signs to each song.

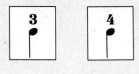

1. Which of these melodies has groups of three ($\frac{3}{4}$ meter)?

   a.   **b.**   **c.**

2. Which of these melodies has groups of four ($\frac{4}{4}$ meter)?

   a.   **b.**   **c.**

3. Which of these melodies starts on an upbeat?

   a.   **b.**   **c.**

4. Which of these melodies starts on a downbeat?

   a.   **b.**   **c.**

5. In which measure do you hear the dotted half note?

   a. (measure one) **b.** (measure two) **c.** (measure three) **d.** (measure four)

6. In which measure do you hear the whole note?

   a. (measure one)   **b.** (measure two)   **c.** (measure three)   **d.** (measure four)

7. Which rhythm do you hear?

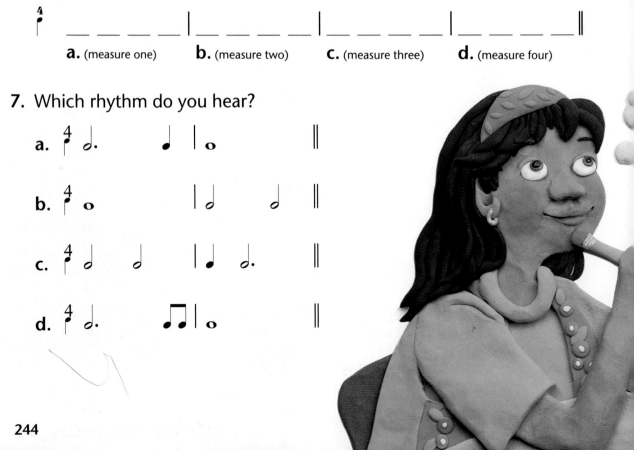

CREATE

Write Ostinato Accompaniments!

Draw these lines on a piece of paper.

$\frac{3}{4}$ __ __ __ | __ __ __ | __ __ __ | __ __ __ :||

Choose from these rhythms to fill in the measures.

Choose an unpitched instrument, such as a drum.

PLAY your ostinato as an accompaniment to "Cuequita de los Coyas" or "Tititorea."

Repeat these steps to create an ostinato in $\frac{4}{4}$ meter. Then play your ostinato as an accompaniment to "Sweep, Sweep Away."

$\frac{4}{4}$ __ __ __ __ | __ __ __ __ | __ __ __ __ | __ __ __ __ :||

Write

Choose a song to sing with an activity you do every day. Write about why you chose that song.

SWEET
BETSY FROM PIKE

American Folk Song
Adapted by Merrill Staton

Verse

D   A7   D

1. Oh, do you re-mem-ber sweet Bet-sy from Pike,
2. 'Twas ear-ly one eve-ning they camped on the Platte,
3. They soon reached the des-ert where Bet-sy gave out,
4. Said Ike, "Ole Pike Coun-ty, I'll go back to you."
5. They camped on the prai-rie for weeks up-on weeks.

D   E7   A7

Who crossed the wide prai-ries with her broth-er Ike?
By the side of the road on a green shad-y flat.
And down in the sand she lay roll-in' a-bout,
Said Bet-sy, "You'll go by your-self if you do.
They swam the wide riv-ers and crossed the tall peaks.

D   F♯m   G   D

With two yoke of ox-en, a big yal-ler dog,
Sweet Bet-sy, sore foot-ed, lay down to re-pose,
When Ike saw sweet Bet-sy he said with sur-prise,
There's no time for plea-sure and no time for rest,
And soon they were roll-in' in nug-gets of gold.

D   A7   D

A___ tall Shang-hai roost-er and one spot-ted hog.
While_ Ike kept the watch o'er his Pike Coun-ty rose.
"You'd_ bet-ter get up, you'll get sand in your eyes."
In___ spite of our trou-bles we'll keep head-in' west."
You___ may not be-lieve it but that's what we're told.

246

Refrain

Hoo - dle dang, fol - de - dye - do, hoo - dle dang, fol - de - day.

Hoo - dle dang, fol - de - dye - do, hoo - dle dang, fol - de - day.

El charro
The Cowboy

Mexican Folk Song
English Version by MMH

Spanish: Es - ta - ba un cha - rro sen - ta - do_____ en las
Pronunciation: es ta βaun cha r̄o sen ta ðo en las
English: A mourn - ful cow - boy was sit - ting_____ on the

tran - cas de un cor - ral._____ ____
tran kas ðe un ko r̄al
rail - ing be - side a cor - ral._____ ____

Su ma - yor - do - mo le di - ce:_____ "No es - tés
su ma yor ðo mo le ði se noes tes
Then came his fore - man to tell him, "Don't be un -

tris - te, Ni - co - las."_____ ____
tris te ni ko las
hap - py Ni - co - las."_____ ____

Unit 5 *Work, Play—and Sing!* **247**

THE WORLD IS A RAINBOW

Words and Music by Greg Scelsa

you, and I'll be me, that's the way we were meant to

be.___ But the world is a mix-ing cup, just

look what hap-pens when you stir it up.

The world___ is a rain - bow,_____

___ with man-y kinds of peo - ple,_____

___ and when we work to-geth - er, it's

such a sight to see. The world is beau-ti-ful__ when we

live in har-mo - ny. La la la la la

ny. la la___ la la la la___la la

All About the DOUBLE BASS

The double bass is the largest member of the string family. Do you know the names of the other instruments in this family?

The double bass is the lowest-sounding string instrument. It usually plays a background part, but its rich sound is very important to the orchestra. In jazz bands, the bass is played **pizzicato,** or plucked.

IN E SHARP

This is a collage by Romare Bearden (1914–1988).
A collage is a work of art made by pasting different
materials, such as paper or cloth, together.

MEET *Milt* Hinton

Milt Hinton has played double bass for nearly sixty years. He has appeared with many great jazz artists such as Louis Armstrong, Charlie Parker, and Benny Goodman. During his long career, Hinton has made more records than any other jazz musician. He is also an excellent photographer.

LISTEN to this great double bass player talk about his career.

WRITE about the part of the interview that you found most interesting. Share your essay with the class.

The double bass can be played like a rhythm instrument in a **slap bass** style. Instead of just plucking the notes, the player also slaps the double bass to create these sounds:

Boom CHUK-A **B**oom CHUK-A
Boom CHUK-A **B**oom **B**oom

Can you say these sounds?

SING the following pattern in a slap bass style.

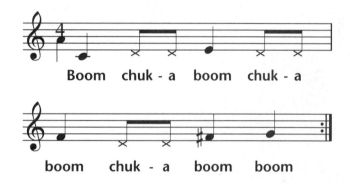

Boom   chuk - a   boom   chuk - a

boom   chuk - a   boom   boom

LISTENING

Three Little Words

from *Trio Jeepy by B. Kalmar and H. Ruby*

LISTEN to Milt Hinton improvise in a slap bass style.

IDENTIFY a familiar song. Raise your hand when you hear Milt Hinton playing it. What is the name of this song?

What's the News?

THE POSTMAN

The whistling postman swings along.
His bag is deep and wide,
And messages from all the world
Are bundled up inside.

The postman's walking up our street.
Soon now he'll ring my bell.
Perhaps there'll be a letter stamped
In Asia. Who can tell?

—*Anonymous*

255

THE WELLS FARGO WAGON

Words and Music by Meredith Willson

O-ho the Wells Far-go wag-on is a-
Wells Far-go wag-on is a-

com-in' down the street, oh please let it be for
com-in' down the street, oh don't let him pass my

me._____ O-ho the Wells Far-go wag-on is a-
door._____ O-ho the Wells Far-go wag-on is a-

com-in' down the street. I wish, I wish I knew what it could
com-in' down the street, I wish I knew what he was com-in'

be.____ I got a box of ma-ple sug-ar on my
for.____ I got some sal-mon from Se-at-tle last Sep-

birth-day._____ In March I got a grey mack-i-
tem-ber._____ And I ex-pect a new rock-in'

WHAT'S THE MESSAGE?

What news have you heard recently? Did you get your news from a letter? Television? Newspaper? Friend?

LISTEN to "I Got a Letter" as you think of getting news that makes you happy.

I Got a Letter

South Carolina
Singing Game

I got a let-ter this morn - ing, Oh, yes;

I got a let-ter this morn - ing, Oh, yes.

Listen to "I Got a Letter" again and guess what kind of news was in each of the four letters. How did the music change to show each different kind of news?

People can express feelings through their paintings.

COMPARE these two paintings.

FIRST DAY OF SCHOOL
Catrin Zipfel, age 10, is from the Federal Republic of Germany.

Courtesy of The U.S. Committee for UNICEF

Courtesy of The U.S. Committee for UNICEF

SAD FAMILY
Jacqueline Menendez Encalade, age 11, is from Ecuador.

During years of slavery, enslaved African Americans sang songs about freedom. Many escaped to freedom by following a secret path north. The chariot in "Good News" stands for a way to travel to freedom.

SING "Good News" to send a message of joy!

GOOD NEWS

African American Spiritual

Good   news!   Char - i - ot's   a - com - in',

Good   news!   Char-i-ot's a-com-in', Good   news!

Char - i - ot's a-com-in', and I   don't want it to leave me be - hind.

The feelings expressed in a piece of music change with the way it's performed. Musical markings tell you how to perform a song.

SING "Good News" three different ways. How do your feelings change?

> > > > >
Good   news!   Char- i - ot's   a - com - in',

Marcato means to sing the notes short, with extra force.

Good   news!   Char- i - ot's   a - com - in',

Staccato means to sing short and light.

Good   news!   Char- i - ot's   a - com - in',

Legato means to sing smoothly.

261

NO BAD

This song is from the Broadway musical *The Wiz*,
based on the story *The Wonderful Wizard of Oz*.

Don't Nobody Bring Me No Bad News

Words and Music by Charlie Smalls

NEWS

But don't no-bod-y bring me ___ no bad ___ news. ___
But don't no-bod-y bring me ___ no bad ___ news. ___
But don't you _____ bring me ___ no bad ___ news. ___

Refrain

No bad news, no bad news.

Don't you ev-er bring me no bad news. ___

'Cause I'll make you ___ an of-fer, child, ___ that you can-not ___ re-fuse,

so don't no-bod-y bring me ___ no bad ___ news. ___ 2. When you're
3. Bring some

(7 times)

___ Don't you bring me ___ no bad news.

HOME, SWEET HOME

"Don't Nobody Bring Me No Bad News" has an ending that sounds very complete, or final. The melody ends on the **tonal center,** or **home tone.** Many melodies start on the home tone, move away from it, and then return. It's often the last pitch of a melody.

Choose a place in your classroom to call home.

MOVE away as you sing "Don't Nobody Bring Me No Bad News." Return home by the end of the song.

LISTENING **March of the Wooden Soldiers**

from *Album for the Young*

by Piotr Ilyich Tchaikovsky

Listen to "March of the Wooden Soldiers" as you pat with the beat.

Listen again, as you march away from your home position. Return home by the end of the final phrase.

"Old Man Moses" also ends on the home tone.

LISTEN to the doctor's advice in "Old Man Moses."

Old Man Moses

African American Game Song

Old man Mo - ses, sick in bed, ___

Called for the doc - tor and the doc - tor said, ___

"Please step for - ward and turn a - round, ___

Do the ho - key po - key and get out of town!" ___

SING "Old Man Moses" to find the words sung on the home tone.

Music with Style

Musical style refers to everything used in a piece of music: rhythms, pitches, tone colors, instruments, and accompaniment. Your clothes also have style.

COMPARE the clothes in these three pictures. Which style would you choose to wear?

1920s

1950s

Art has different styles, too. How are these two paintings different?

EDWARD VI, WHEN DUKE OF CORNWALL

Hans Holbein, the court painter, finished this realistic portrait painting in 1543. It shows Edward when he was six years old. He became King of England four years later.

The Metropolitan Museum of Art, the Jules Bache Collection, 1949 (49.7.31)

1990s

© 1993 The Andy Warhol Foundation for The Visual Arts, Inc.
Courtesy of Leo Castelli Gallery

MARILYN

Andy Warhol finished this silkscreen and oil painting of Marilyn Monroe in 1964.

meet *Midori*

Performers such as Midori have their own style. When she was your age, she practiced the violin three to four hours a day! At eleven, she made her first appearance with the New York Philharmonic. Midori's mother was also a violinist. Midori remembers being surrounded by music as she grew up in Japan. Now she travels all around the world giving concerts and making recordings. She loves making music and hopes to do this all her life.

LISTENING

Caprice in A Minor excerpts

by Niccolò Paganini

"Caprice" was written for the violin about 100 years ago.

LISTENING MAP *Listen to Midori play "Caprice" as you follow this listening map.*

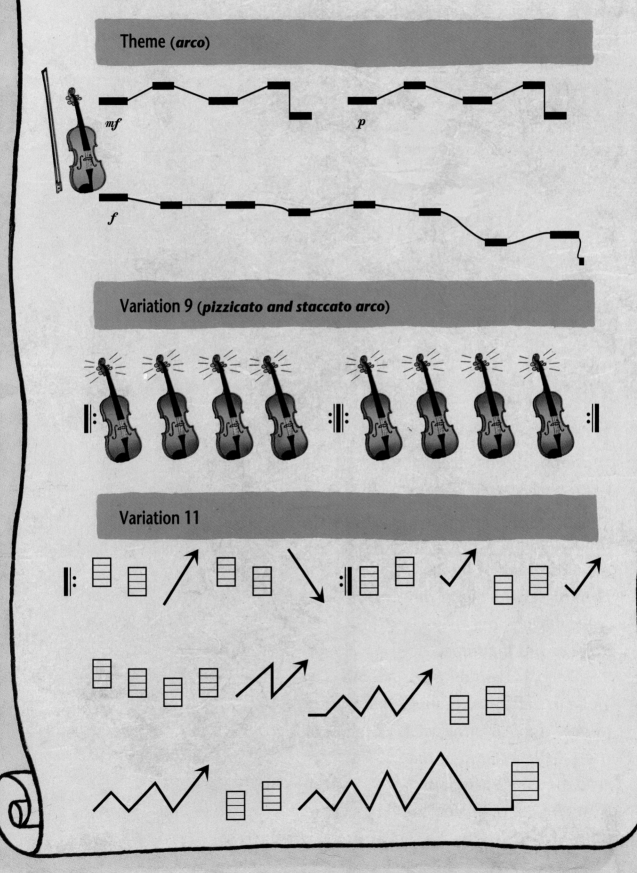

Theme (*arco*)

Variation 9 (*pizzicato and staccato arco*)

Variation 11

LOOK at these two instruments. Why might they sound different?

violin

LISTENING

Variations excerpts
by Andrew Lloyd Webber

"Variations" was recently written by Andrew Lloyd Webber. It has a more modern musical style than the "Caprice in A Minor." Both pieces start with the same melody, but they don't sound the same.

The high sound of the violin in the "Caprice in A Minor" is much different from the low sound of the cello used in "Variations." How else are the pieces different?

cello

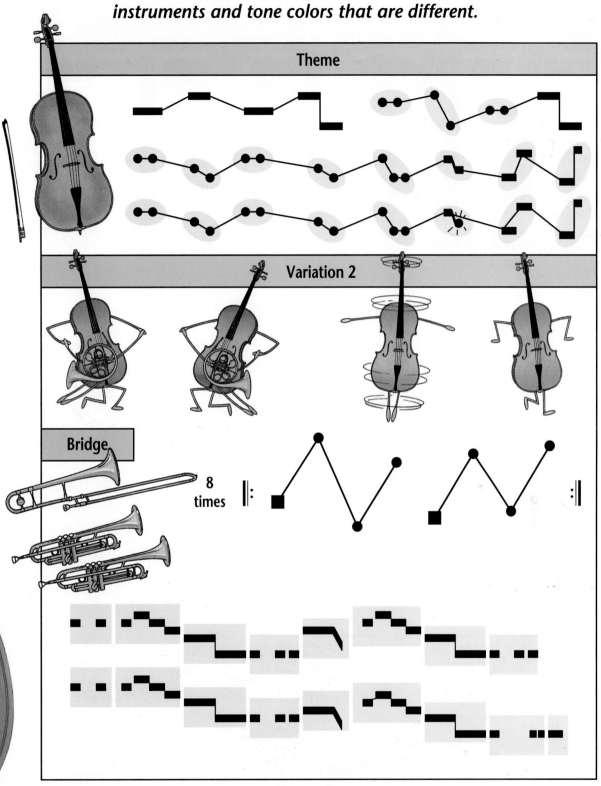

COMPARE the "Caprice in A Minor" with "Variations." Think about the instruments, rhythms, and accompaniment.

FIND YOUR WAY

H⦿ME

LISTEN to "Killy Kranky" to find the home tone.

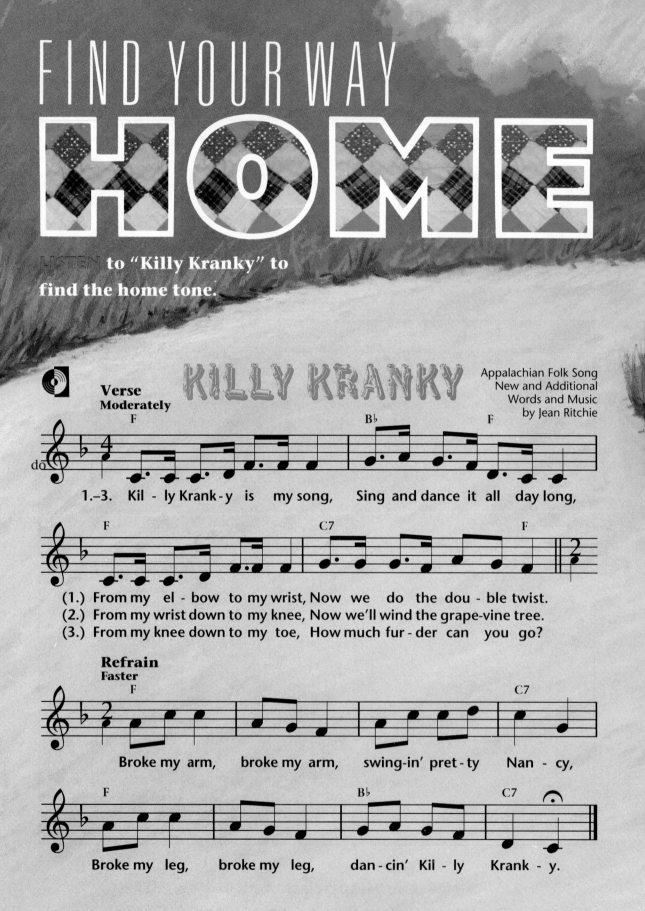

KILLY KRANKY

Appalachian Folk Song
New and Additional
Words and Music
by Jean Ritchie

Verse
Moderately

1.–3. Kil - ly Krank - y is my song, Sing and dance it all day long,

(1.) From my el - bow to my wrist, Now we do the dou - ble twist.
(2.) From my wrist down to my knee, Now we'll wind the grape-vine tree.
(3.) From my knee down to my toe, How much fur - der can you go?

Refrain
Faster

Broke my arm, broke my arm, swing-in' pret - ty Nan - cy,

Broke my leg, broke my leg, dan - cin' Kil - ly Krank - y.

The home tone in "Killy Kranky" is *do*. It's in the first space. Which phrase ends on *do*?

Appalachian dulcimer

"Killy Kranky" is a game song from Appalachia, a mountain area in the southeastern United States.

Meet
JEAN RITCHIE

Jean Ritchie wrote some of the words for "Killy Kranky." She was raised in the Cumberland Mountains of Kentucky. She was the youngest of 14 children. As a child, she "would worry that there would sometimes come an evening when they wouldn't sing!" Her family sang songs from their English, Scottish, and Irish ancestors.

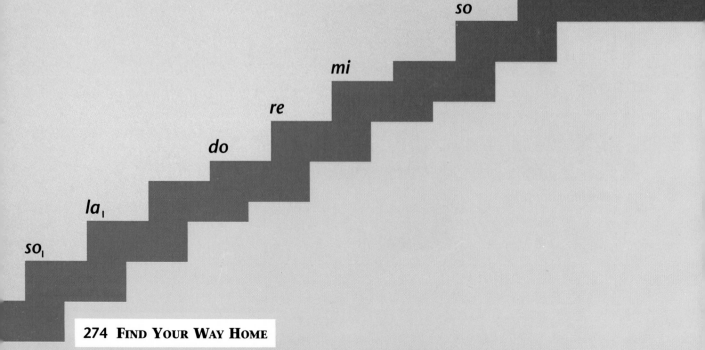

Zudio was a word used in the 1920s. It meant a two-step dance movement.

LOOK at the pitch stairs and name all of the pitch syllables in the song "Zudio." Then name the home tone.

la

so

mi

re

do

la₁

so₁

LISTEN to "Zudio" and hum the
home tone.

ZUDIO

Traditional African American Street
Game Adapted by Janet McMillion

Dm   Gm   Dm

1. Here we go Zu - di-o, Zu - di-o, Zu - di-o.
2. Step __ back Sal - ly, __ Sal - ly, __ Sal - ly, __
3. Go - in' down the al - ley, __ al - ley, __ al - ley, __

Dm   Gm   Dm

Here we go Zu - di - o,
Step __ back Sal - ly, } all night long. ____
Go - in' down the al - ley,

DANCE the "Zudio" movement as you sing
the song.

MUSICAL SIGNS

Remember the music sign called *repeat*? When two phrases are exactly the same, you don't have to write them twice. You can write the phrase once, then add a repeat sign to each end (‖: :‖). The refrain from "Killy Kranky" can be written using a repeat sign and a first and second ending.

Refrain
Faster

Broke my arm,   broke my arm,   swing-in' pret-ty   Nan - cy,
Broke my leg,   broke my leg,

dan - cin' kil - ly   krank - y.

The repeat sign in the **first ending** tells you to go back to the beginning. Then, skip over the first ending to the measures in the **second ending.**

SING the refrain, touching the measures in order as you sing them.

276

DANCING "KILLY KRANKY"

Many people in the southern Appalachian Mountains, where "Killy Kranky" comes from, are skilled at crafts. They weave baskets, patterns in cloth, even dances!

This picture shows a section of a weaving dance.

"Señor Don Juan de Pancho" comes from the southwestern part of the United States. Many people there speak both Spanish and English.

LISTEN to "Señor Don Juan de Pancho" to find a section in Spanish and a section in English.

Señor DON JUAN de Pancho

New Mexico
Folk Song
English Version
by MMH

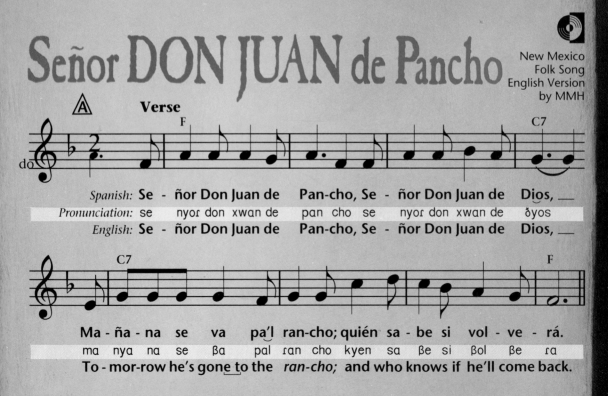

Ⓐ **Verse**

F   C7

Spanish: **Se - ñor Don Juan de Pan-cho, Se - ñor Don Juan de Dios, __**
Pronunciation: se nyor don xwan de pan cho se nyor don xwan de ðyos
English: **Se - ñor Don Juan de Pan-cho, Se - ñor Don Juan de Dios, __**

C7   F

Ma - ña - na se va pa'l ran-cho; quién sa - be si vol - ve - rá.
ma nya na se βa pal ɾan cho kyen sa βe si βol βe ɾa
To - mor-row he's gone to the *ran-cho;* **and who knows if he'll come back.**

B **Refrain**

Shoo fly, don't both-er me, Shoo fly, don't both-er me,

Shoo fly, don't both-er me, I be-long to Com-pa-ny D.

**SING this new melody with words, following
the first and second endings.**

Shoo, fly! Go a - way. way.

do re re re mi do

**LISTEN to "Señor Don Juan de Pancho" and
sing this new melody along with the refrain.**

A MESSAGE OF
GOOD NEWS!

Send a message of good news through art, music, and dance.

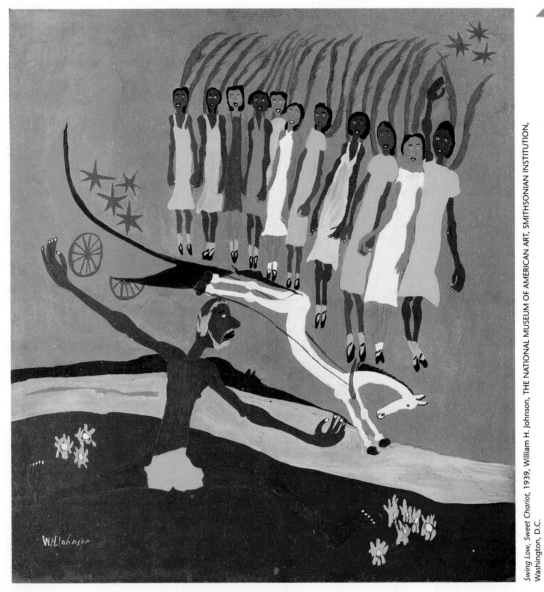

Swing Low, Sweet Chariot, 1939, William H. Johnson, THE NATIONAL MUSEUM OF AMERICAN ART, SMITHSONIAN INSTITUTION, Washington, D.C.

SWING LOW, SWEET CHARIOT

In this painting, artist William H. Johnson used long, flowing figures that seem to blend into one another. His choice of warm, rich colors helps to send a comforting message.

SING "Good News" to send a comforting message.

Good News

African American Spiritual

crescendo

Good news! Char - i - ot's a - com - in',

Good news! Char-i-ot's a-com-in', Good news!

Char-i-ot's a-com-in', and I don't want it to leave me be - hind.

COMPARE "Good News" on page 260 with "Good News" on this page. How are the notes different?

The letter name for the note in the first space is F.

PLAY the tinted notes on bells. Then sing the song, playing A, G, and F on the tinted notes.

A   G   F

PLAY the melody at the bottom of page 279 on these bells.

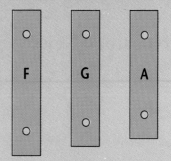

Some people in New Mexico perform a dance with "Señor Don Juan de Pancho."

Learn the dance by walking this rhythm through shared space.

Right, left, right,   left, right, left.

You've just learned the **ranchero step**!

DANCE the ranchero step, moving counterclockwise during the A section.

WALK four steps toward the middle of the circle and clap on the last step during the B section.

WALK four steps out and clap on the last step. Circle in place for four beats, then stamp, stamp, clap, clap.

Sing Your Message

SING "I Got a Letter," pretending to be happy, sad, mad, or excited about the news in your letter.

I GOT A LETTER

South Carolina
Singing Game

I got a let-ter this morn-ing, Oh, yes.

Oh, yes.

READ the last pitch syllable and name the tonal center.

How are the two phrases alike? How are they different?

CREATE your own phrases using these four pitches.

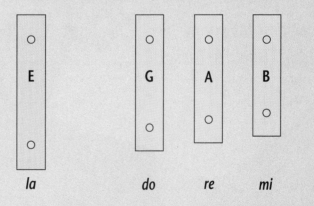

PLAY the rhythm of "I Got a Letter" on any of these bells. Did you end on the tonal center?

You just made your own melody!

Scat singing is made up of nonsense syllables that don't mean anything. Scat was created when jazz singers listened to jazz instruments and used their voices to imitate the sounds they heard.

Spotlight on ELLA FITZGERALD

Ella Fitzgerald was an American jazz singer known for her scat singing. She started singing as a teenager to earn extra money for her family. When she was eighteen, she wrote and sang her first hit song, "A-Tisket, A-Tasket."

Doodle

Wah-wah

It Don't Mean a Thing if It Ain't Got that Swing

LISTENING

by Duke Ellington and Irving Mills

LISTEN to Ella Fitzgerald scat sing in this piece. What scat syllables does she sing?

You can learn to scat sing, too! Listen to "Old Man Moses" to hear scat singing with a song you know.

Choose one of the following scat patterns and sing it in place of the words *Do the hokey pokey and get out of town.*

Imitate the clarinet by singing:

doodle, doodle, doodle, det, det, det!

Imitate the trombone:

wah-wah, wah-wah, wah-wah, woo, woo, wah!

Imitate the trumpet by pinching your nose and singing:

Daba, daba, daba, daba, dat, dat, dot!

CREATE your own scat melodies.

DANCE YOUR MESSAGE

The song "Señor Don Juan de Pancho" comes from New Mexico, where the ranchero step is popular.

PERFORM the ranchero step as you listen to "Señor Don Juan de Pancho."

Form a double circle with a group in your class.

CHOOSE one of the three body-facings pictured for your group.

Front-to-front: partners facing each other

CREATE a dance using the ranchero step. Start your dance in your chosen body-facing. End your dance in a different body-facing.

Side-to-side: partners shoulder-to-shoulder

Back-to-back: partners facing away from each other

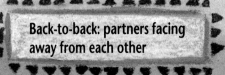

In the Appalachian Mountains, the clogging step is popular. The clogging step was originally brought to North America from the British Isles.

PAT this clogging rhythm.

Right, left, right,   left, right, left.

Now step the rhythm.

SING "Killy Kranky" as you perform the clogging step during the verse.

MUSIC

Can you dance?
I love to dance!
Music is my happy chance.
Music playing
In the street
Gets into
My hands and feet

Can you sing?
I love to sing!
Music, like a bird in Spring,
With a gold
And silver note
Gets into
My heart and throat.

Can you play?
I'd love to play!
Practice music everyday—
Then you'll give
The world a chance
To dance and sing,
To sing and dance.

—*Eleanor Farjeon*

These dancers belong to the Billy Bob Cloggers of North Carolina.

SONGS MAKING THE HEADLINES

What songs do these
headlines suggest?

EXTRA!

SALLY STEPS BACK

MAIL COMES BEFORE NOON

JUAN FLEES INSECTS

CHARIOT REPLACES POST OFFICE TRUCK

DANCING DOCTOR HEALS SENIOR CITIZEN

Say some of these headlines in staccato, marcato, or legato style. Then sing some of the songs using these expressive markings. Which style do you like better? Why?

CHECK IT OUT

1. How is this music sung?

   a. staccato   **b.** legato   **c.** marcato

2. How is this music sung?

   a. staccato   **b.** legato   **c.** marcato

3. How does this music end?

   a. on the tonal center   **b.** away from the tonal center

4. How does this music end?

   a. on the tonal center   **b.** away from the tonal center

5. Which melody do you hear? Is the tonal center of
   that melody *do* or *la₁*?

CREATE

Express Yourself

Create a piece of music with first and second endings. Draw these lines on a piece of paper.

Choose some of these rhythms.

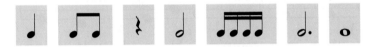

Play your piece on instruments. Then perform it using some of the following expressive markings.

p

mf

f

slow

staccato

marcato

fast

legato

Write

Think of some good news that you received recently. Write a newspaper article about the event. Include a catchy headline.

Waltzing Matilda

Music Adapted by Marie Cowan
Words Adapted from A. "Banjo" Paterson

Verse

1. Once a jol - ly swag - man camp'd__ by a bil - la - bong,
2. Down came a jum - buck to drink__ at that bil - la - bong,
3. Up came the stock - man, mount - ed on his thor - ough - bred,
4. Up jumped the swag - man, sprang in - to the bil - la - bong,

Un - der the shade of a coo - li - bah tree, And he
Up jumped the swag - man and grabbed him with glee, And he
Down came the troop - ers,__ one,__ two, three.
"You'll nev - er catch me a - live,"__ said he, And his

sang as he watched and wait - ed till his bil - ly boiled,
sang as he shoved that jum - buck in his tuck - er - bag,
"Who's that jol - ly jum - buck you've got in your tuck - er - bag?"
ghost may be heard as you pass__ by that bil - la - bong,

"You'll come a waltz - ing Ma - til - da with me."

Refrain

Waltz - ing Ma - til - da, waltz - ing Ma - til - da,

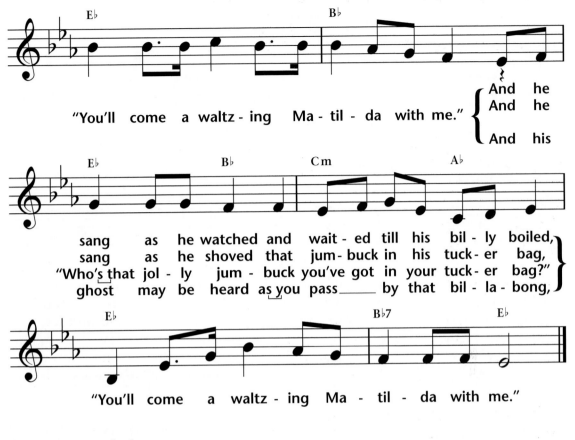

"You'll come a waltz - ing Ma - til - da with me."

{
And he
And he
And his
}

sang as he watched and wait - ed till his bil - ly boiled,
sang as he shoved that jum - buck in his tuck - er bag,
"Who's that jol - ly jum - buck you've got in your tuck - er bag?"
ghost may be heard as you pass____ by that bil - la - bong,

"You'll come a waltz - ing Ma - til - da with me."

Swagman—a hobo

Billabong—a water hole in a dried-up riverbed

Billy—a tin can used as a kettle to boil water

Waltzing Matilda—the bundle on a stick carried by a swagman

Jumbuck—a small lamb

Tuckerbag—a knapsack

Stockman—a person who owns or works with livestock

Good-bye My Riley O

African American Song
from the Georgia Sea Islands
Collected and Adapted by Lydia A. Parrish

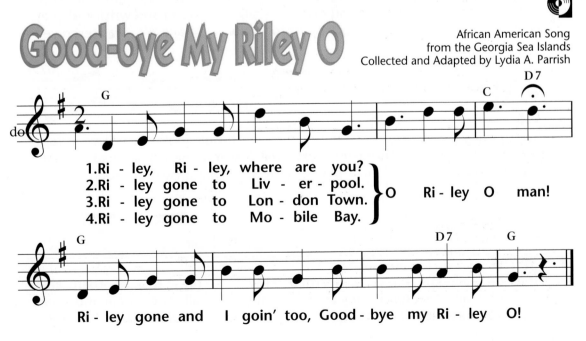

1. Ri - ley, Ri - ley, where are you?
2. Ri - ley gone to Liv - er - pool.
3. Ri - ley gone to Lon - don Town.
4. Ri - ley gone to Mo - bile Bay.

} O Ri - ley O man!

Ri - ley gone and I goin' too, Good - bye my Ri - ley O!

THE
Kindergarten Wall

Freely

Verse

Words and Music by J. McCutcheon

1. When I was a lit - tle kid not so long a - go,
(2.) first, ___ sec - ond, third ___ grade, fourth ___ grade, ___ too,
3. Late - ly I've been wor - ried as I look a-round and see,

I had to learn a lot of stuff I did - n't ev - en know:
Where I had to learn the big ___ things the big ___ kids ___ do:
An aw - ful lot of grown-ups act - ing fool-ish as can be.

How to dress my - self and tie my shoes, how to jump a rope,
To ___ add, sub - tract, and mult - i - ply, read and write and play,
Now I know there's lots of things to know I have-n't mas-tered yet,

How to smile for a pic - ture with-out look - ing like a dope.
How to sit in a lit-tle un-com-fort-a-ble desk for near - ly half a day.
But it seems there's real im - por - tant stuff that grown-ups soon for-get.

But of all the things I learned, my fav'-rite of them all,
But of all the things they taught me, of all the great and small,
So I'm sure we'd all be bet - ter off if we would just re - call

298

Was a lit-tle poem hang-ing on the kin-der-gar-ten wall:
Still my fav'-rite was the po-em on the kin-der-gar-ten wall:
That ___ lit-tle poem hang-ing on the kin-der-gar-ten wall:

Refrain

Of all you learn here, re-mem-ber this the best:

Don't hurt each oth-er and clean up your mess;

Take a nap ev'-ry day, wash be-fore you eat,

Hold hands, stick to-geth-er, look be-fore you cross the street;

And re-mem-ber the seed in the lit-tle pa-per cup,

First the root goes down and then the plant grows up. 2. Was

The Recording Studio

Can you imagine a world without music? Watching your favorite television program or listening to the radio would be a very different experience.

Much of the music you enjoy on radio and television is produced in a recording studio. This is a place where musicians record their work.

A studio usually has many rooms. In one room, the performance room, the musicians perform. In another, the control room, specially trained engineers work to make the recording.

THE PERFORMANCE ROOM

The performance room is soundproof. This keeps the room very quiet while the music is being played. Microphones pick up the sound of the voices or instruments. These sounds are recorded on special equipment located in the control room. When the performers wear headphones, they can hear the music that is being recorded. They can also hear what the people in the control room are saying to them.

THE CONTROL ROOM

The control room has many pieces of equipment. The most important piece is the tape recorder. The size of the tape on this machine is bigger than that on a home tape recorder. It is wider and comes on very large reels.

The different sounds of the recording are put together on a large control, or mixing, board.

The electronic speakers allow the people in the control room to hear what is being recorded. Other equipment helps to make the final recording sound wonderful.

All the rooms have glass walls or large windows. In this way, the performers can see one another. With their headphones, they can also hear one another.

WHO WORKS THERE?

The people who work in a recording studio have many skills.

One person is the engineer. The engineer understands how all the equipment works. Other people help the engineer. Some of the jobs include setting up the microphones and mixing the final recording.

CALENDAR

January shivers,
February shines,
March blows off the winter ice,
April makes the mornings nice,
May is hopscotch lines.

June is deep blue swimming,
Picnics are July,
August is my birthday,
September whistles by.

October is for roller skates,
November is the fireplace,
December is the best because
        of sleds
                and snow
                        and Santa Claus.

—*Myra Cohn Livingston*

305

FROM SEA SHINING TO SHINING SEA

Katharine Lee Bates wrote the words to "America, the Beautiful" while visiting Colorado.

America, the Beautiful

Music by
Samuel Ward
Words by
Katharine Lee Bates

O beau-ti-ful for spa-cious skies, For am-ber waves of grain.

For pur-ple moun-tain maj-es-ties, A - bove the fruit-ed plain.

A - mer-i-ca! A - mer-i-ca! God shed His grace on thee,

And crown thy good with broth-er-hood, From sea to shin-ing sea.

Yankee Doodle Boy

Words and Music by George M. Cohan

I'm a Yan - kee Doo - dle Dan - dy,

A Yan - kee Doo - dle, do or die;

A real live neph - ew of my Un - cle Sam,

Born on the Fourth of Ju - ly.

I've got a Yan - kee Doo - dle sweet - heart,

She's my Yan - kee Doo - dle joy.

Yan - kee Doo - dle came to Lon - don, just to ride the po - nies,

I am a Yan - kee Doo - dle boy.

Woody Guthrie was a composer and folk singer. His songs often describe the beauty of places he visited.

This Land Is Your Land

Words and Music
by Woody Guthrie

Refrain

This land is your land, _____ This land is my land, _____ from Cal-i-for-nia _____ to the New York is-land, _____ From the red-wood for-est _____ to the Gulf Stream wa-ters; _____ This land was made for you and me. _____

Verse

1. As I was walk-ing _____ that rib-bon of high-way, _____
2. I've roamed and ram-bled _____ and I fol-lowed my foot-steps _____
3. When the sun comes shin-ing _____ and I _____ was stroll-ing _____

I saw a-bove me _____ that end-less sky-way. _____
to the spar-kling sands of _____ her dia-mond des-erts, _____
and the wheat fields wav-ing _____ and the dust clouds roll-ing, _____

I saw be-low me _____ that gold-en val-ley, _____
And all a-round me _____ a voice was sound-ing, _____
As the fog was lift-ing _____ a voice was chant-ing, _____

Go back to the beginning and sing to the end
(Da Capo al Fine)

This land was made for you and me. _____
"This land was made for you and me." _____
"This land was made for you and me." _____

America

Music by Henry Carey
Words by Samuel F. Smith

My coun-try 'tis of thee, Sweet land of

lib-er-ty, Of thee I sing.

Land where my fa-thers died, Land of the Pil-grim's pride,

From ev'-ry _____ moun-tain-side, Let _____ free-dom ring.

Read the words to these songs. Do you think they
are scary? What makes them playful as well?

My Good Old Man

Southern American Folk Song

1. Where are you go - ing,
2. What will you buy there,
3. Bush - el will kill you, } my good old man?
4. What for to die, ____
5. Why will you haunt me,

Where are you go - ing,
What will you buy there,
Bush - el will kill you, } my sug - ar, my lamb?
What for to die, ____
Why will you haunt me,

Best old man in the world. _____

Spoken:
(1) To market.
(2) Bushel of eggs.
(3) Don't care if it does.
(4) So I can haunt you.
(5) So I can always be near you.

Halloween Night

Words and Music
by Doris Parker

Refrain
𝆑 Dm

Bet - ter watch out, it's Hal - low - een night.

Dm | A7 | Dm

Look at all the spook - y sights. ___

Dm

Bet - ter watch out it's Hal - low - een night.

Dm | A7 | Dm

End (Fine)

Look at all the spook - y sights. ___

Name sound effects you could use to create a spooky feeling. Share your sound effects with the class as you sing the song.

Verse

1. Skel - e - tons, let's have some fun.
2. Witch - es, too, what can you do?
3. Gob-lins and ghosts, how can you fly?

When I count to eight, you must be done. ___
When I count to eight, you must be through. _
When I count to eight, come down from the sky. ___

Go back to the beginning and sing to the end
(Da Capo al Fine)

p

One two three four five six seven eight.

HARVEST TIME

The tradition of having a celebration at harvest time is thousands of years old. In the United States, Thanksgiving is an important harvest celebration. People everywhere celebrate the earth's gifts.

Gather 'Round

Words and Music
by Margaret C. duGard

Raise your voice with _ joy - ous _ ring - ing, Gath - er 'round hear _

chil - dren sing - ing. Ding, dong, ding, ring - a - ling,

Ding, dong, ding, ring - a - ling. Give thanks and sing, Give

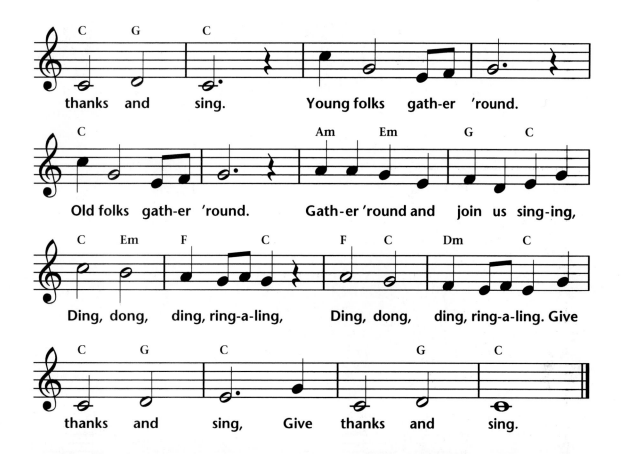

thanks and sing. Young folks gath-er 'round.

Old folks gath-er 'round. Gath-er 'round and join us sing-ing,

Ding, dong, ding, ring-a-ling, Ding, dong, ding, ring-a-ling. Give

thanks and sing, Give thanks and sing.

Thanksgiving Day Is Here

Come gather 'round the table,
    Thanksgiving Day is here.
When we give thanks for family,
    And friends who we hold dear.
We'll talk of that day long past,
    When pilgrims came to stay.
And how the Native peoples
    Gave help to them each day.
And just like us, they joined hands
    And sang a song in praise,
Of love for friends and family,
    And bounteous harvest days.

—*Constance Andrea Keremes*

Sukkot is a Jewish celebration of the fall harvest. A long time ago, farmers built huts in their fields to stay in during harvest. Today, families build small shelters to celebrate that tradition. "Hag Asif" describes the time of Sukkot.

HAG ASIF
Harvest Time

Words and Music
by S. Levy Tannai
English Version by L. Koulish

Refrain

Hebrew: חַג אָ - סִיף, חַג אָ - סִיף | - בֶּה - יִרְ כֵּן | - וְ סִיף יוֹ - כֵן.

Pronunciation: xag a sif xag a sif ken yir be və xen yo sif

English: **Har-vest time, har-vest time. Gath-er in the gold-en wheat.**

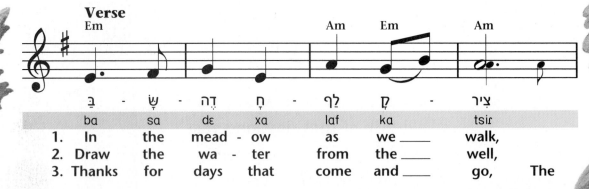

Verse

בַּ - שָׂ - דֶה חָ - לַף קָ - צִיר

ba sa de xa laf ka tsir

1. In the mead - ow as we ___ walk,
2. Draw the wa - ter from the ___ well,
3. Thanks for days that come and ___ go, The

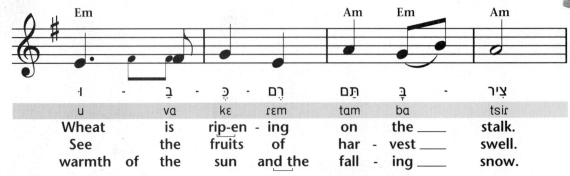

וּ - בַ - כֶּ - רֶם תַּם בַּ - צִיר

u va kε rεm tam ba tsir

Wheat is rip-en - ing on the ___ stalk.
See the fruits of har - vest ___ swell.
warmth of the sun and the fall - ing ___ snow.

וְ - עַ - תָּה עִם בֹּא הַסְ - תָו
və a ta im bo has tav
Wield the scythe and cut the grain,
Build the suk - kot tall and strong.
Thanks for our food and the crops that grow, The

חַג אָ - סִיף נָ - חֹג בְּ - שִׁיר.
xag a sif na xog bə shir
Au - tumn sea - son's here a - gain.
Join our hands in dance and ____ song.
love we share and the friends we ____ know.

WINTER FEST

When winter comes, people
enjoy the beauty of ice and snow.
In northern Japan, families build special
snow huts for a Snow Hut Festival.

YUKI
SNOW

Japanese School Song
English Version by MMH

F

Japanese:	ゆ	—	き	や	こん	こん		あ	られ	や	こん	こん
Pronunciation:	yu		ki	ya	kon	kon		a	ɾa ɾe	ya	kon	kon
English:	**Snow**		**is**	**fall - ing,**	*kon,*	*kon.*		**Hail**	**is fall - ing,**		*kon,*	*kon.*

F ... **C7**

ふっ	て	わ	ふっ	て	わ	ずん	ずん	つ	も	る
fut	te	wa	fut	te	wa	zu n̩	zu n̩	tsu	mo	ɾu
Snow	**fall - ing,**		**snow**	**drift-ing,**		**down __ down __**		**hail**	**and**	**snow.**

F

や	—	ま	も	の	は	ら	も	わ	た	ぼ	し	か	ぶ	り
ya		ma	mo	no	ha	ɾa	mo	wat	ta	bo	shi	ka	bu	ɾi
Hills __ wear-ing snow white cot-ton								**caps and cloaks of drift-ing snow.**						

B♭ **F** ... **C7** **F**

か	れ	き	の	こ	ら	ず	は	な	が	さ	く
ka	ɾe	ki	no	ko	ɾa	zu	ha	na	ga	sa	ku
There	**on the**		**cold, bare branch-es**				**snow flow'rs are**		**in**		**bloom.**

318

The Sleigh

Words by Ivor Tchervanow
Music by Richard Kountz

pp—mf 1. Light - ly fly - ing o'er the snow, with a

pp 2. All the world a blank - et white of _____

hey, hah, hah, hah, ho, hah, ho, With

snow so cold and crisp and light, with

3rd time to Coda ⊕

sleigh - bells ring - ing, bright - ly sing - ing, mer - ri - ly we go.

sharp winds blow-ing, we are go-ing, on - ward through the night.

D.C. (Verse 1) al Coda

f *f*

Hey - a - o - la! Hey - a - o - la!

Coda ⊕ *f* *f*

Ho, hal - lo! Mer - ri - ly on we go. Ho, hal - lo!

Mer - ri - ly on we go. Hah, hah, hah,

hah, hah, hah, hah, hy - ah, hah, hah, hah,

hy-ah, hah, hy-ah, hah, hy-ah, hah, hy-ah, hah, hah, _____ Ha-ya-ha!

EIGHT DAYS OF LIGHT

The story of Hanukkah tells how a little oil kept the holy lamps in Jerusalem burning for eight days. The holiday is celebrated by lighting candles. Eight candles are placed in a candleholder called a *menorah*. Each night, a ninth candle is used to light one more candle. On the last night of Hanukkah, all of the lights burn brightly together.

O, Hanukkah

Jewish Folk Song
English Version by MMH

Yiddish: אוֹי אַ ,כָּה - נוּ - חַ אוֹי ,חַ - נוּ - כָּה, אַ יוֹן - טָאב אַ שֵיי - נֶער אַ

Pronunciation: o xɑn u kɑ o xɑn u kɑ ɑ yɔn tɛf ɑ she nɛɹ ɑ

English: O Ha-nuk-kah, O Ha-nuk-kah, a beau-ti-ful sea-son, a

Yiddish: לוס - טי - קער ,אַ - פְרֵיי - לֶע - כֶער, נִי - טָאֶ נָאֶך אַ - זוֹי - נֶער.

Pronunciation: lus tig ɛr ɑ frɛ lix ɛr ni to nɔx ɑ zɛɪ nɛɹ

English: joy-ous hap-py fes-ti-val un-like an-y oth-er.

Yiddish: מִיר, לָן - שְׁפִּי דְלֶעך אִין דְרֵיי נַאכְט לֶע אַ

Pronunciation: ɑ lə nɑxt in dɹed lɑx shpi lən miɹ

English: Spin-ning, turn-ing drey-dls and good things to eat;

320

The Eight Days of Hanukkah

Words and Music by
George David Weiss

Verse

Solo Dm — A 7

"One" is for the tem-ple walls that did-n't fall._____

Group A 7 — Solo Dm

(Did-n't fall.) "Two" is for the men who fought, God

A 7 — Group — Solo Gm

bless 'em all._____ (Bless 'em all.) "Three" is for the oil they

Gm — Dm — E

found, e-nough for just one day. "Four" is for the

E — A 7 B♭7 A 7 — Group

mir-a-cle that came their way; it burned for eight days.

Solo Dm — A 7

"Five" is for the hope and faith that would-n't die._____

Group A 7 — Solo Dm

(Would-n't die.) "Six" is for the To-rah scrolls that

Gm — Group — Solo D 7

still sur-vive._____ (Still sur-vive.) "Sev-en" is for all the

songs in hon - or of them.____ Num - ber

"Eight" a prayer and "A - men."_____

Refrain

Eight days of Ha - nuk - kah, eight hap - py nights.

Eight days to cel - e - brate the fes - ti - val of lights.

Eight gifts at Ha - nuk - kah, what mem - 'ries they raise,____

____ of those eight won - der - ful days.___

1. _____ Let's all count, count the ways.____

2. _____ Of those eight won - der - ful days.____

People in many parts of the world celebrate Christmas on December 25. This holiday honors the birth of Jesus. In the United States, we share many different holiday songs and customs that express joy. Some people shout "Hallelu!" What other words do you know that express the same feeling?

Wasn't That a
MIGHTY
Day?

African American Folk Song

324

Children, Go Where I Send Thee

African American Carol

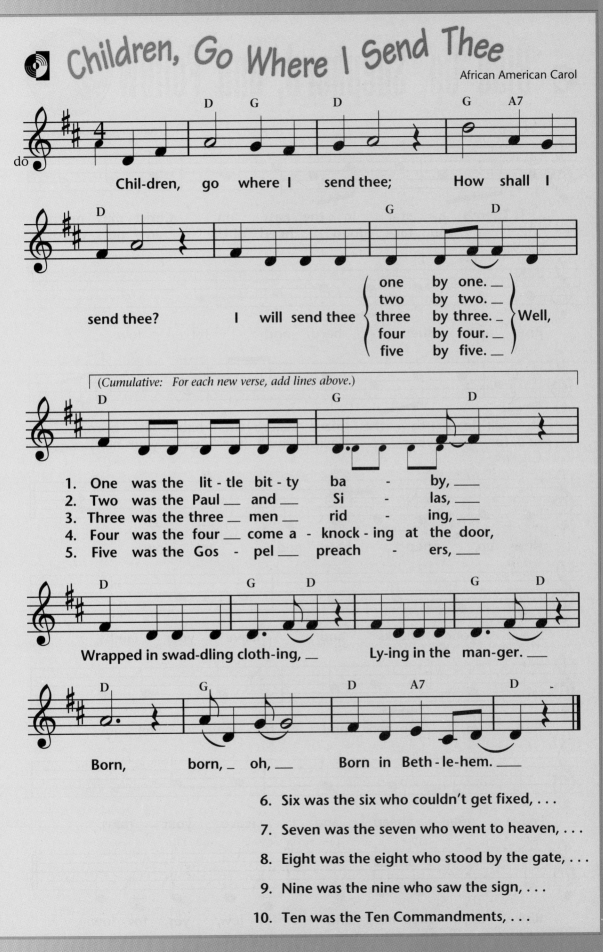

Chil-dren, go where I send thee; How shall I send thee? I will send thee
{
one by one. __
two by two. __
three by three. __
four by four. __
five by five. __
} Well,

(Cumulative: For each new verse, add lines above.)

1. One was the lit-tle bit-ty ba - by, ___
2. Two was the Paul __ and __ Si - las, ___
3. Three was the three __ men __ rid - ing, ___
4. Four was the four __ come a - knock - ing at the door,
5. Five was the Gos - pel __ preach - ers, ___

Wrapped in swad-dling cloth-ing, __ Ly-ing in the man-ger. ___

Born, born, __ oh, __ Born in Beth-le-hem. ___

6. Six was the six who couldn't get fixed, . . .

7. Seven was the seven who went to heaven, . . .

8. Eight was the eight who stood by the gate, . . .

9. Nine was the nine who saw the sign, . . .

10. Ten was the Ten Commandments, . . .

Rise Up, Shepherd, and Follow

African American Spiritual

Verse

Solo

1. There's a star in the East on Christ-mas morn,
2. If you take good___ heed of the an-gel's words,

Chorus

Rise up, shep - herd, and fol - low.

Solo

It will lead to the place where the babe is born,___
You'll for - get your___ flocks, you'll for - get your herds,___

Chorus

Rise up, shep - herd, and fol - low.

Leave your flocks and leave your lambs,

Rise up, shep-herd, and fol - low, fol - low.

Leave your sheep and leave your rams,

Rise up, shep-herd, and fol - low, yes, fol - low.

Refrain

Fol - low, fol - low,

Rise up, shep - herd, and fol - low.

Fol - low the star of Beth - le - hem,

Rise up, shep - herd, and fol - low.

LISTENING

Great Day in December by C. Jeter

In this music, one man sings the words that tell
the Christmas story. He has a very high voice.
Four other men sing with him in the background.
How is the story in this song the same or different
from others you have heard?

Members of the Boys Choir of Harlem

The Christmas story tells of three kings who brought gifts. This poem is about one of those men. His name was Balthazar. Why does the poet think Balthazar was special?

Carol of the BROWN KING

Of the three Wise Men
Who came to the King,
One was a brown man,
So they sing.

Of the three Wise Men
Who followed the Star,
One was a brown king
From afar.

They brought fine gifts
Of spices and gold
In jeweled boxes
Of beauty untold.

Unto His humble
Manger they came
And bowed their heads
In Jesus' name.

Three Wise Men,
One dark like me—
Part of His
Nativity.

—Langston Hughes

Members of African American churches often answer the preacher. The people say "Hallelu!" or "That's right!" or "Amen!"

AMEN

African American Spiritual
Additional Words by MMH

Swing *mf*

A - men, A - men,

A - men, A - men, A - men, men. See the (1.) ba - by,
(2.) Moth - er,
(3.) Shep - herds,

Ly - ing in the man - ger,
Sing -in' to the ba - by,
Come to see the ba - by, } One Christ - mas morn - ing,

All

A - men, A - men, A - men.
A - men, A - men, A - men.
A - men, A - men, A - men. Sing it soft - er now, —

p first time only

All

A - men, A - men,

ff last time only

A - men, A - men, A - men, Sing it strong - er now, — men.

Group may continue with "Amen" throughout solo part.   Celebrations *Christmas* **329**

Yuletidings

The ideas in this carol come from a part of the Bible called the Book of Psalms. When you sing this song, let your glad feelings show!

Joy to the World

Music by Lowell Mason
English Poem by Isaac Watts

Joy to the world! the Lord is come.

Let earth re ceive her King.

Let ev' - ry ___ heart ____ pre - pare _ Him _ room. ____

And heav'n and na-ture _ sing, And _ heav'n and na-ture _ sing,

And _ heav'n, _ and heav'n _____ and na - ture sing.

"Deck the Hall" describes the joyful custom of decorating for Christmas. The song comes from Wales, where singing contests are held the week before Christmas.

Deck the Hall

Welsh Carol

Gaily

1. Deck the hall with boughs of hol-ly,
2. See the blaz-ing yule be-fore us, Fa la la la la, la la la la,
3. Fast a-way the old year pass-es,

'Tis the sea-son to be jol-ly,
Strike the harp and join the cho-rus, Fa la la la la, la la la la,
Hail the new, ye lads and lass-es,

Don we now our gay ap-par-el,
Fol-low me in mer-ry mea-sure, Fa la la la la la, la la la,
Sing we joy-ous all to-geth-er,

Troll the an-cient yule-tide car-ol,
While I tell of yule-tide trea-sure, Fa la la la la, la la la la.
Heed-less of the wind and weath-er,

Here is an imaginative version of how the story
of the birth of Jesus was passed along.

Do You Hear What I Hear?

Words and Music by
Noel Regney and Gloria Shayne

1. Said the night-wind to the lit-tle lamb,
(2. Said the) lit-tle lamb to the shep-herd boy,
(3. Said the) shep-herd boy to the might-y king,
(4. Said the) king to the peo-ple ev-'ry-where,

(Echo in verses 1–3)

Do you see what I see?___ (Do you see what I see?)
Do you hear what I hear?___ (Do you hear what I hear?)
Do you know what I know?___ (Do you know what I know?)
Lis-ten to what I say!___

'Way up in the sky, lit-tle lamb,
Ring-ing through the sky, shep-herd boy,
In your pal-ace warm, might-y king,
Pray for peace___ peo-ple ev-'ry-where,

(Echo in verses 1–3)

Do you see what I see?___ (Do you see what I see?) A
Do you hear what I hear?___ (Do you hear what I hear?) A
Do you know what I know?___ (Do you know what I know?) A
Lis-ten to what I say!___ The

star, a star, Danc-ing in the night, with a
song, a song, High a-bove the tree, with a
Child, a Child, shiv-ers in the cold; Let us
Child, the Child, sleep-ing in the night; He will

This carol was first sung many years ago in France.
Which words in the song make the sound of a flute?
Which ones make the sound of a drum?

Pat-a-Pan

English Version
by Merrill Staton

1. Wil - lie take your lit - tle drum, Rob-in bring your flute and come.
2. When the lit - tle child was born long a - go that Christ-mas morn,
3. Now we cel - e-brate this day on our in - stru-ments we play.

Play a joy - ous tune to - day.
Shep-herds came from fields a - far, { Tu-re-lu-re - lu, pat-a-pat-a - pan,
Let our voi - ces loud-ly ring, }

Play a joy - ous tune to - day on this joy - ous hol - i - day.
Shep-herds came from fields a - far guid-ed by the shin-ing star.
Let our voi - ces loud-ly ring, as our song and gifts we bring.

The farmer in this song was preparing his piglets for the holiday. Read Verses 3 and 4 to find out what happened!

From HOUSE to HOUSE

In England many years ago, friends greeted each other at holiday time with "Was haile!" These words meant "Be healthy!" When carolers sang from house to house, their neighbors gave them a hot drink to warm themselves.

Here We Come A-Wassailing

English Carol

Verse

1. Here we come a - was-sail - ing   a - mong the leaves so green, ___
2. are not dai - ly beg - gars that beg from door to door. We
3. bless the mas-ter of this house, like-wise the mis-tress too, And

Here we come a - wan-d'ring so   fair ___ to be   seen;
are your neigh-bor's chil - dren whom you have seen be - fore.
all the lit - tle chil-dren that   round the ta - ble go.

336

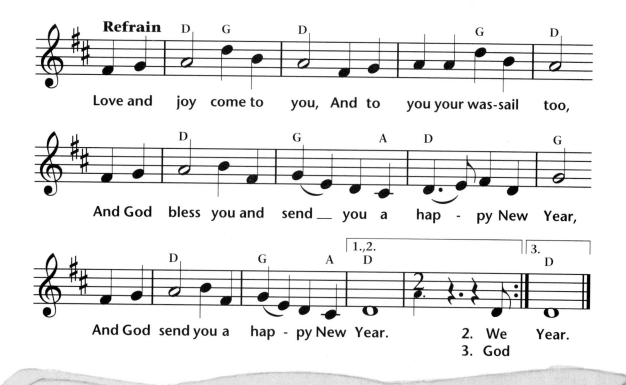

Love and joy come to you, And to you your was-sail too,

And God bless you and send ___ you a hap - py New Year,

1.,2.

3.

And God send you a hap - py New Year.

2. We Year.
3. God

from
CAROL

This poem from *The Wind in the Willows* is about a chorus of mice who visit their neighbors, the Rat and the Mole.

Villagers all, this frosty tide,
Let your doors swing open wide.
Though wind may follow, and snow beside,
Yet draw us in by your fire to bide;
Joy shall be yours in the morning!

Here we stand in the cold and the sleet,
Blowing fingers and stamping feet,
Come from far away to greet—
You by the fire and we in the street—
Bidding you joy in the morning!

—Kenneth Grahame

Everybody Says *Freedom*

Martin Luther King, Jr., Day celebrates the birthday of Dr. King. He fought for equality and justice for African Americans and people everywhere.

WOKE UP THIS MORNING

Freely

Freedom Song

Woke up this morn-ing with my mind ——— stayed on free - dom. ———

Woke up this morn-ing with my heart ——— stayed on free - dom. ———

Woke up this morn-ing with my soul _____ stayed on free - dom. __

Hal-le - lu, hal-le-lu, hal-le - lu, hal-le-lu, hal-le - lu - jah.

I'm gon-na walk, talk, _ sing, shout, _ hal - le - lu __ I got my

mind on free-dom. Walk, talk __ sing, shout, _ clap my hands and keep my

mind on free-dom. Walk, talk, _ sing, shout, _ clap my hands. _

LISTENING

I'm on My Way to Freedom Land

Adaptation of a traditional song

During the 1960s, songs about equality for African Americans became popular. Songs like this one made everyone aware of Dr. King's dream.

DESCRIBE **what you think a place called Freedom Land would be like.**

Be My Valentine

A favorite Valentine's Day custom is sending cards or flowers. Some messages aren't signed so that the name of the sender is a secret. Do you think this song is for a friend?

Never Gonna Be Your Valentine

Words and Music by Linda Worsley

1. I don't wan-na be your val - en - tine,
2. I'm not gon-na be your val - en - tine,
3. I might wan-na be your val - en - tine,

I don't wan-na be your val - en - tine,
I'm not gon-na be your val - en - tine,
I might wan-na be your val - en - tine,

Don't wan-na be your val - en - tine to - day!
You're not the kind of val - en - tine I like!
Don't tell a soul, 'cause you know ver - y well

Oh, no, I don't wan-na be your val - en - tine,
Oh, no, I'm not gon-na be your val - en - tine,
If all my friends knew I was your val - en - tine,

I don't wan-na be your val - en - tine,
I'm not gon-na be your val - en - tine,
They'd tease me and call me "Val - en - tine,"

Pack up your val - en - tine and go a - way!
Pack up your val - en - tine and take a hike!
That's why you have to prom-ise not to tell!

You nev - er let me win at games,
You won't share this, you won't lend that.
But you're so mean, you won't keep still!

You laugh at me and call me names,
Won't e - ven let me pet your cat!
You'll tell them all, I know you will!

So e - ven if you beg and plead and whine, _____
And yet you bor - row ev' - ry - thing that's mine! _____
So e - ven though I think you're real - ly fine, _____

I'm nev - er gon-na be your val - en - tine! _____

Irish Eyes Are Smiling

We celebrate St. Patrick's Day with parades, shamrocks, and by wearing green. Green is a reminder of the Irish land.

LISTENING St. Patrick's Day

by Leo Rowsome

Leo Rowsome was a famous Irish piper. He learned to make and play the pipes from his father and grandfather. Bagpipes are filled with air. The air is pushed through a pipe to make its sound. The Irish pipes are played without blowing the air—instead the player pumps the air into the bag with his or her arm.

This Irish folk song is about a man who works hard and is proud of it.

The Wee Falorie Man

Irish Folk Song
Collected by
David Hammond

do

F

1. I am the wee Fa - lo - rie man,
2. I am a good old work - in' man,

Dm   F

A rat - tlin', rov - in' I - rish - man,
Each day I car - ry my wee tin can, A

F

I can do all that ev - er you can, For
large pen - ny bap and a clipe _____ of ham,

Dm   C7   F

I am the wee Fa - lo - rie man.
I am a good old work - in' man.

Spring Breezes

Shavuot, a Jewish festival, celebrates the spring harvest. Farmers of ancient Israel brought the first fruits to Jerusalem to give thanks. Shavuot is a time of sharing with friends and family.

HAG
SHAVUOT
Festival of First Fruits

Traditional Israeli
Holiday Song
English Version by MMH

Hebrew: חַג שָׁ-בוּ-עוֹת חַג שָׁ-בוּ-עוֹת הִ עוֹת-בוּ-שָׁ חַג הַ -
Pronunciation: xag sha vu ot xag sha vu ot xag sha vu ot hi
English: **Hag Sha-vu-ot,** *hag sha-vu-ot,* **hag sha-vu-ot** the __

Hebrew: נֶה זֶה בָּא. עַל רָא -שֵׁי -נוּ זֵר פְּרָ -חִים
Pronunciation: ne ze ba al ɾɔ she nu zeɾ pɾɑ xim
English: fruit is here. We shall dress our hair with gar - lands

Hebrew: בְּ -יָ -דֵי -נוּ רִים-כּוּ-בִּ רִים-כּוּ-בִּ.
Pronunciation: bə ya de nu bi ku ɾim bi ku ɾim
English: car - ry first fruits __ in our hands. in our hands.

344

Cherry trees and their delicate blossoms are a special part of Japanese spring celebrations.

Sakura

Cherry Blossoms

Japanese Folk Song
English Version by MMH

Japanese: さくら　さくら　やよいの　そらは
Pronunciation: sa ku ɾa　sa ku ɾa　ya yo i no　so ɾa wa
English: **Cher-ry tree,　Cher-ry tree!　Cher-ry blos-soms　ev'-ry - where.**

みわたす　かぎり　かすみか　くもか
mi wa ta su　ka gi ɾi　ka su mi ka　ku mo ka
Far as an - y　eye can _ see.　Mist and beau-ty　fill the _ air,

におい ぞ　いずる　いざや　いざや
ni o i zo　i zu ɾu　i za ya　i za ya
Love-ly blos-soms　scent the _breeze. Come with me,　come with me,

み　に　ゆ　か　ん
mi　ni　yu　ka　ŋ
Let _____ us　go _____ and　see.

This short Japanese poem is called a *haiku*.

**Ashes my burnt hut
But wonderful the cherry
Blooming on the hill.**

–Hokushi

Voices of the Earth

The Pygmies live in the rain forest in the Central African Republic. The forest gives them food, clothing, warmth, and a feeling of friendship.

This is a song and dance that celebrates the earth and all growing things. *Ema* means mother. The rest of the words have no special meaning, but are there just to sing.

Ema, Ma

Pygmy Dance Song

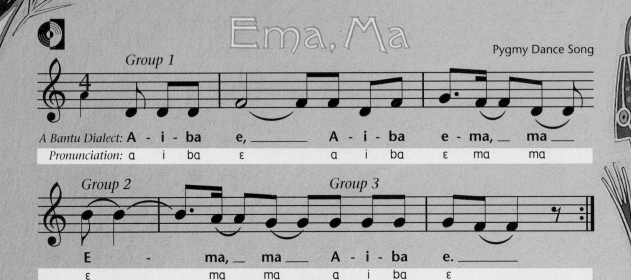

Group 1

A Bantu Dialect: **A - i - ba   e, _____   A - i - ba   e - ma, _ ma _____**
Pronunciation: ɑ   i   bɑ   ɛ   ɑ   i   bɑ   ɛ   mɑ   mɑ

Group 2   **Group 3**

E - _ ma, _ ma _ A - i - ba   e. _____
ɛ   mɑ   mɑ   ɑ   i   bɑ   ɛ

From Morning Night to Real Morning

Voices of the rain forest collected by Steven Feld

Before the sun comes up, the rain forest is alive with the rhythm of insects, tree frogs, and dripping leaves. Listen for these sounds. You will also hear the voices of more than 150 different kinds of birds singing.

DANCE OF THE ANIMALS

I throw myself to the left,
I turn myself to the right,
I am the fish
Who glides in the water, who glides,
Who twists himself, who leaps.
Everything lives, everything dances, everything sings.

The bird flies,
Flies, flies, flies,
Goes, comes back, passes,
Mounts, hovers, and drops down.
I am the bird.
Everything lives, everything dances, everything sings.

The monkey, from bough to bough,
Runs, leaps, and jumps,
With his wife, with his little one,
His mouth full, his tail in the air:
This is the monkey, this is the monkey.
Everything lives, everything dances, everything sings.

—Pygmy Song

"All Living Things" reminds us that all life on Earth is connected.

NAME the living things in this song.

ALL LIVING THINGS

Words and Music by W. Jay Cawley

Verse

1. All liv-ing things _____ need the air to breathe, __
2. All liv-ing things _____ need the warm sun-shine, __
3. All liv-ing things _____ need to have a home, __

Need the sky __ up a-bove, __ the earth be-neath their feet. __
Need the cool __ sum-mer breeze, __ that blows on down the line. __
Need a place _ to rest __ their heads, __ a pur-pose of their own. __

For the fish-es in __ the o-cean and the birds that sing, __
For the ap-ples in __ the or-chards and the flow-ers in __ the spring, __
We must live __ to-geth-er __ so let us dance and sing, __

This world ____ is the home __ of liv-ing things. things.

1.,3. D *End*   **2.** D

Interlude

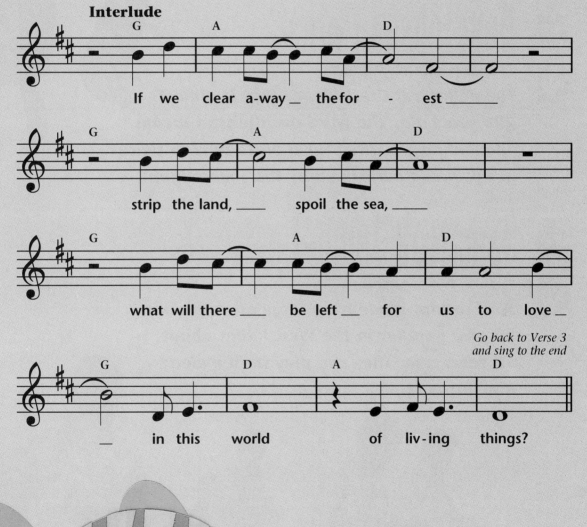

If we clear a-way _ the for - est _____

strip the land, ____ spoil the sea, ____

what will there ____ be left ___ for us to love _

*Go back to Verse 3
and sing to the end*

_ in this world of liv-ing things?

Summer Folk *Festival*

Summer folk festivals celebrate many traditions. They include everything from polkas to barbershop quartets.

Doudlebska Polka

LISTENING

Traditional Czech Polka

*The polka is a Czech dance that is almost 200 years old. The word **doudlebska** means "double clap." Listen for a place to clap twice in this polka performed by the Shenanigans.*

Jamaican Jump-Up

LISTENING

by H. C. Mon Solomon

Steel drums, made from large oil containers, became popular in the West Indies about 50 years ago. They can play both melody and harmony.

IN THE GOOD OLD SUMMERTIME

Music by George Evans
Words by Ron Shields

In the good old sum - mer - time.____ In the good old

sum - mer - time.____ Stroll - ing through the shad - y

lanes, with your ba - by mine.____ You

hold her hand and she holds yours. And that's a

ver - y good sign.____ That she's your toot - sey

woot - sey in the good old sum - mer - time.____

LISTENING

In the Good Old Summertime

Music by George Evans
Words by Ron Shields

Only one person sings the melody in a barbershop quartet. Three other people sing harmony.

LISTEN to a barbershop quartet sing. How is it different from the way you sing this song?

Folk dancing is popular at summer festivals.
Try this dance with a partner.

Cotton-Eyed Joe

American Dance Song

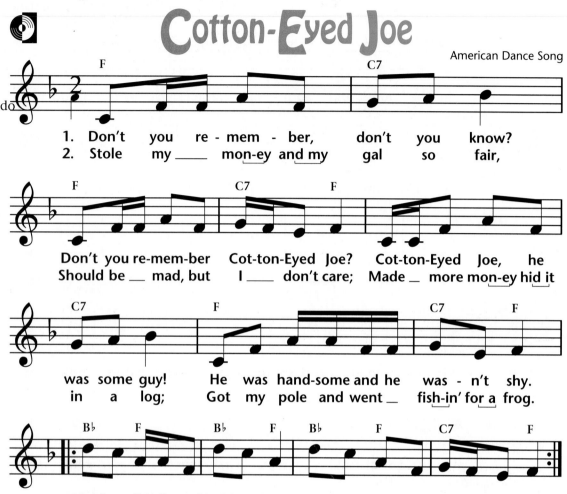

1. Don't you re - mem - ber, don't you know?
2. Stole my ____ mon-ey and my gal so fair,

Don't you re-mem-ber Cot-ton-Eyed Joe? Cot-ton-Eyed Joe, he
Should be __ mad, but I ____ don't care; Made __ more mon-ey hid it

was some guy! He was hand-some and he was - n't shy.
in a log; Got my pole and went __ fish-in' for a frog.

Hold my fid-dle and hold my bow, watch me dance like Cot-ton-Eyed Joe.

Brush

Kick

The rhythm of these Spanish words will help you keep the steady beat. As you sing this game song, pass a stone around the circle.

ACITRÓN

Spanish Stone-Passing Game

Spanish: A - ci - trón de un fan - dan-go, zan-go, zan-go, sa-ba - ré.
Pronunciation: ɑ si tɾon de um fan dan go san go san go sa βɑ ɾe

Sa-ba - ré de far - an - de-la, con su tri-qui, tri-qui tran.
sa βɑ ɾe ðe faɾ an de la kon su tɾi ki tɾi ki tɾan

Grandma's Feather Bed

Words and Music by Jim Connor

Verse

1. Now when I was a lit- tle bit- ty boy Just up off___ of the

floor, We used to go out to Grand- ma's house

ev'- ry month end or so.___ We'd have chick- en pie___ and

coun- try ham, and home - made but- ter on the

bread. But the best thing a - bout Grand - ma's house was a

great big feath - er bed.

Refrain

It was nine feet high and six feet wide and

soft as a down-y chick. It was made from the feath-ers of

for-ty 'lev-en geese, took a whole bolt of cloth for the

tick. It-'d hold eight kids and four____ hound dogs and the

pig-gy we took from the shed. We did-n't get much sleep, but we

had a lot of fun on Grand-ma's feath-er bed.

2. And after supper we'd sit around the fire
and the old folks bit the shoe.
And my Pa would talk about the farm and the war
and my Granny'd sing a ballad or two.
And I'd sit and listen and watch the fire till
the cobwebs filled my head.
The next thing I know I'll wake up in the mornin'
In the middle of the old feather bed.
Refrain

3. Well I love my Ma, I love my Pa
I love Granny and Grandpa too.
I been fishin' with my Uncle
and I wrassle with my Cousin
I even kissed Aunt Lou (Phew!)
But if I ever had to make a choice
I guess it ought to be said.
That I'd trade them all plus the gal down the road
For Grandma's feather bed.
Refrain

More Songs to Read

Beats with Sounds and Silences

PLAY this pattern with the beat as you sing "Telephone Song."

Play   Play

Beats with sound   Beats with silence

Telephone Song

American Singing Game

"Hey, Char - ley!" _____ "I think I hear my name!" _

"Hey, Char - ley!" _____ "I think I hear it a - gain!"

"You're want - ed on the tel - e - phone!"

"If it is - n't Ma - ry I'm not ___ at home!"

Chorus

With a rick - tick - tick - e - ty tick, _____ Oh yeah! __

With a rick - tick - tick - e - ty tick, _____ Oh yeah.

356

High and Low, Loud and Soft

SAY your name in different ways.

HIGH

LOW

LOUD ▷ SOFT

Chatter with the Angels

African American Spiritual

Chat-ter with the an - gels soon in the morn - ing,

Chat-ter with the an - gels all day long. I hope to

join that band and chat-ter with the an - gels all day long.

Reading Rhythm

quarter note	eighth notes	quarter rest
(one sound)	(two sounds)	(no sound)

STEP patterns that include quarter notes, eighth notes, and quarter rests. Then clap the rhythm of "Only My Opinion" as you say the words.

Is a caterpillar ticklish?

Well, it's always my belief

That he giggles as he wiggles

Across a hairy leaf.

—*Monica Shannon*

Sing and Play with *Do Re Mi*

LOOK in each song below for measures that are alike.

mi

re

do

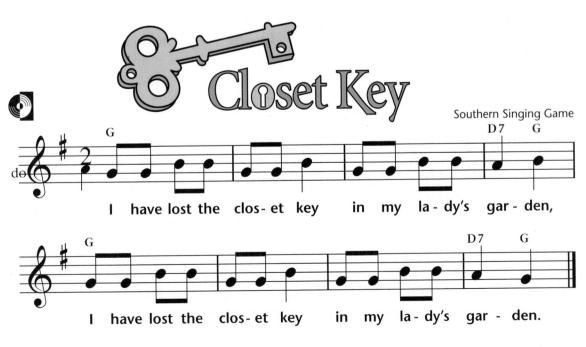

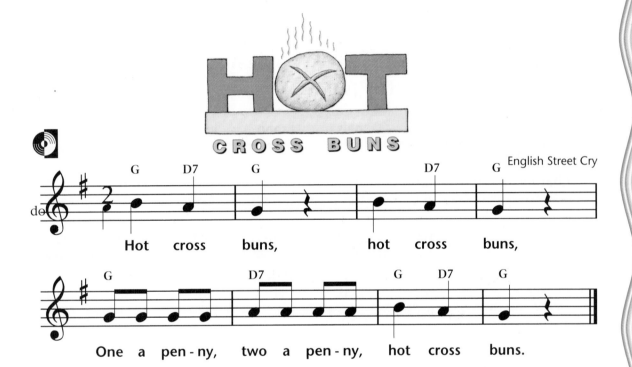

One Beat or Two?

WALK with the beat. Then skate to sounds that
are two beats long.

SING "Chatter with the Angels" and pat with
the beat. Find words that are two beats long.
Then do the same with "Jubilee."

4 Chat-ter	with the	an-	gels	soon	in	the	morn-	ing,

Chat-ter	with the	an-	gels	all	day	long. _____

I _____	hope _____	to	join	that	band	and

Chat-ter	with the	an-	gels	all	day	long. _____

2 All	out	on	the	old rail-	road,	All	out	on	the	sea; _____

All	out	on	the	old rail-	road,	Far	as	I	could	see. _____

Swing and turn,	Ju-	bi- lee,	Live and learn,	Ju-	bi- lee.

STEP and play the pattern below with
"Jubilee."

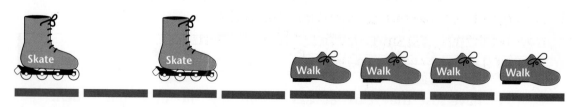

360

Find the Form

WHO BUILT THE ARK?

African American Spiritual

Refrain *Leader* / *Group*

G / D 7

Who built the ark? No - ah, No - ah,

Leader / *Group*

G / D 7 / G *End*

Who built the ark? Broth - er No - ah built the ark.

Verse *All*

G / G

1. Now didn't old No - ah build the ark?_____
2. He built it long, both wide and tall,_____
3. Now in come the an-i - mals two by two,_____

G / D 7 / G

Built it out of a hick - o - ry bark._____
Plen ty of room for the large_____ and small._____
Hip-po- po-ta- mus and_____ kang - a - roo._____

Now in come the animals. . .

4. . . .three by three, Two big cats and a bumblebee.*

5. . . .four by four, Two through the window and two through the door,

6. . . .five by five, Four little sparrows and the redbird's wife,

7. . . .six by six, Elephant laughed at the monkey's tricks,

8. . . .seven by seven, Four from home and the rest from heaven.*

9. . . .eight by eight, Some were on time and the others were late,

10. . . .nine by nine, Some was a-shouting and some was a-crying.

11. . . .ten by ten, Five black roosters and five black hens,

12. Now Noah says, "Go shut that door, The rain's started dropping and we can't take more."*

Sing refrain after verses 4, 8 and 12 only.

Name That Rhythm

READ this rhythm. Name the song, then play the game.

Farfallina
Butterfly

Italian Folk Song
English Version by MMH

G   D7

Italian: Far-fal-li-na   tut-ta bian-ca   vo-la, vo-la,   non si stan-ca.
Pronunciation: far fal li na   tut ta byang ka   vo la vo la   non si stang ka
English: Far-fal-li-na,   with your white wings, fly a-way, do   not sit still. _

G   D7   G

Vo-la   li,   vo-la la,   po-si po-sa   so-pra un fiore.
vo la   li   vo la la   po si po sa   so praun fyore
Fly-ing here,   fly-ing there,   on a flow-er   rest a   while.

Reading *So*

Name the three pitches you
have been reading in songs.

so

In this song you will
use a new pitch, *so*.

do

do   re   mi   so

**SING these patterns with pitch syllables.
Find them in the song below.**

1.   2.   3.

do   do   do

SING the song with pitch syllables.

Matarile

Mexican Folk Song

do

		D				A 7		D	

Spanish: 1.¿Qué   quiere us‐ted?   Ma‐ta‐   ri‐le,   ri‐le,   ri‐le.
Pronunciation: ke   kyeɾe   u   steð   ma   ta   ɾi   le   ɾi   le   ɾi   le
English: 1.What   do   you   want?   Ma‐ta‐   ri‐le,   ri‐le,   ri‐le.

Quie‐ro   sal‐tar,   Ma‐ta‐   ri‐le,   ri‐le,   ron.
kye   ɾo   sal   taɾ   ma   ta   ɾi   le   ɾi   le   ɾon
I   want to   jump,   Ma‐ta‐   ri‐le,   ri‐le,   ron.

2. Quiero marchar, . . .
   kye ɾo maɾ chaɾ
   I want to march, . . .

3. Quiero correr, . . .
   kye ɾo ko ĩeɾ
   I want to run, . . .

Finding a New Pitch

LISTEN to the song. Identify
the new pitch.

CORAL

Folk Song

1. O sail-or come a-shore. What have you brought for me?
2. Did not take it from the ground, nor pick it from a tree;

Red cor-al, white cor-al, cor-al from the sea.
Lit-tle in-sects made it in the storm-y, storm-y sea.

The new pitch in this song is *la*.

In "Great Big House," *do* is in a different
place. Where are *re mi so* and *la*?

la

GREAT BIG HOUSE

Louisiana Play Party Song

1. Great big house in New Or - leans, For - ty sto - ries high; ___
2. Went down to the old mill stream, To fetch a pail of wa - ter;
3. Fare thee well, my dar - ling girl, Fare thee well, my daugh - ter;

Ev' - ry room that I been in, Filled with chick - en pie.
Put one arm a-round my wife, The o - ther 'round my daugh-ter.
Fare thee well, my dar - ling girl, with the gold - en slip - pers on her.

Equal or Unequal?

Our Washing Machine

Our washing machine went whisity whirr,
Whisity, whisity, whisity whirr.
One day at noon it went whisity click,
Whisity, whisity, whisity click.
Click grr, click grr, click grr, click.
Call the repairman.
Fix it quick!

—*Patricia Hubbell*

I Bought a Dozen New-Laid Eggs

I bought a dozen new-laid eggs
Of good old Farmer Dickens;
I hobbled home upon two legs
And found them full of chickens.

—*Mother Goose*

Melodic Direction

MOVE your hands to show the melodic direction
of the words *Shake them 'simmons down.*

'Simmons

Alabama Singing Game

1. Cir - cle   left,
2. Cir - cle   right,   } do oh, do oh,   { Cir - cle   left,
                                            Cir - cle   right, }   do oh, do oh,

Cir - cle   left,
Cir - cle   right, }   do oh,   do oh,   Shake   them   'sim - mons   down!

3. Balance all, . . .   5. 'Round your corners, . . .
4. 'Round your partners, . . .   6. Prom'nade all, . . .

Unequal Rhythms

You know that ♩ usually gets one beat and is equal to ♪♪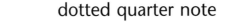

Remember that a dot after a note makes it longer,
so ♩. = ♪♪♪

In ⁶₈ meter, each beat is as long as one of these rhythms.

♩.	dotted quarter note
𝄽.	dotted quarter rest
♪♪♪	three eighth notes
♩ ♪	quarter note + eighth note

READ the rhythm of "Juan Pirulero."

Juan Pirulero

New Mexican Folk Song

Spanish: Es - te es el jue - go de Juan Pi - ru - le - ro;
Pronunciation: es tes el xwe go ðe xwan pi ɾu le ɾo
English: This is the game ___ of Juan Pi - ru - le - ro;

Que ca - da quien a - tien - da a su jue - go.
ke ka ða kyen a tyen da su xwe go
Eve - ry - one lis - ten, learn how to play it.

366

Low *So* and Low *La*

Low *so* and low *la* are found below *do*.

FIND these two patterns in the song, then sing the song.

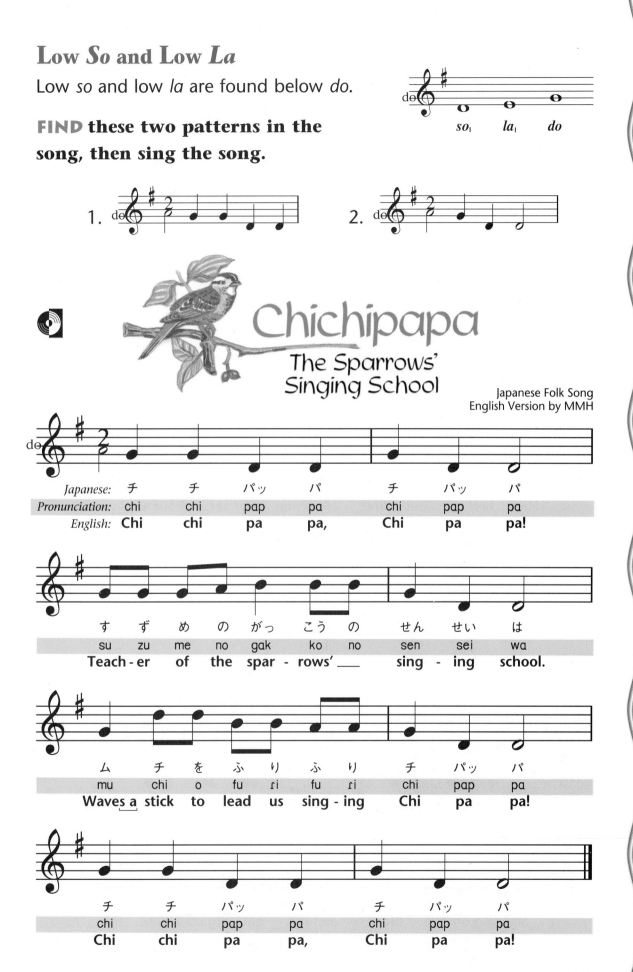

Chichipapa
The Sparrows' Singing School

Japanese Folk Song
English Version by MMH

Japanese:	チ	チ	パッ	パ	チ	パッ	パ
Pronunciation:	chi	chi	pap	pa	chi	pap	pa
English:	**Chi**	**chi**	**pa**	**pa,**	**Chi**	**pa**	**pa!**

す	ず	め	の	がっ	こう	の	せん	せい	は
su	zu	me	no	gak	ko	no	sen	sei	wa
Teach-er	**of**	**the**	**spar-rows'** __				**sing-ing**	**school.**	

ム	チ	を	ふ	り	ふ	り	チ	パッ	パ
mu	chi	o	fu	ri	fu	ri	chi	pap	pa
Waves a stick		**to**	**lead**	**us**	**sing-ing**		**Chi**	**pa**	**pa!**

チ	チ	パッ	パ	チ	パッ	パ
chi	chi	pap	pa	chi	pap	pa
Chi	**chi**	**pa**	**pa,**	**Chi**	**pa**	**pa!**

Read Low *So* and Low *La*

SING these two songs. Both have low *so* and one also has low *la*. *Do* is in the first space.

SCOTLAND'S BURNING

Traditional Round

Scot-land's burn-ing, Scot-land's burn-ing, Look out! Look out!

Fire! fire! fire! fire! Pour on wa - ter, Pour on wa - ter.

One, Two, Three O'Leary

Children's Game Song

1.–2. One, two, three O' Lea - ry, I saw lit - tle Ma - ry

1. Sit - ting on a drom - e - dar - y, eat - ing choc'-late fish - es.
2. Sit - ting on a bas - ket - er - y, eat - ing jel - ly ba - bies.

Play Four Sounds to a Beat

PLAY this accompaniment as you sing "Frog Went A-Courtin'."

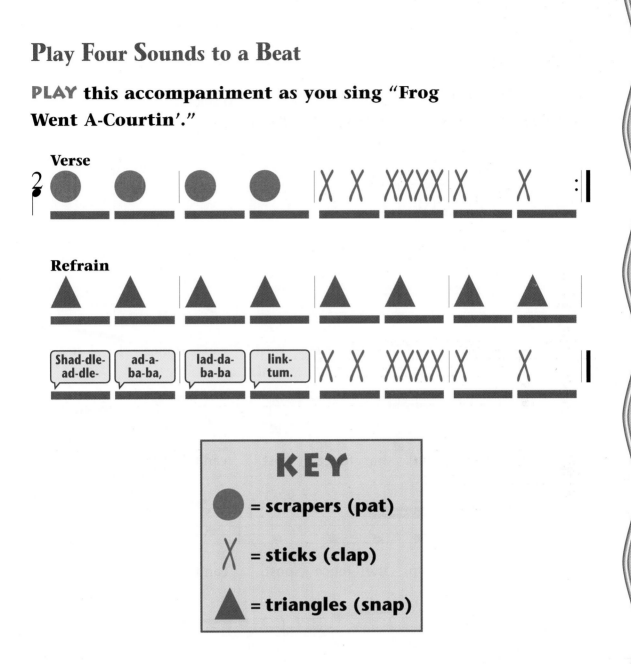

KEY

● = scrapers (pat)

X = sticks (clap)

▲ = triangles (snap)

Read Phrases with Low *So*

SING these phrases with pitch syllables. Then find these phrases in "The Old Sow's Hide."

Read Sixteenth Notes

LOOK for the sixteenth notes as
you read the rhythm of this song.

CHICKEN ON THE FENCE POST

Play-Party Song

Chick - en on the fence post, can't dance Jo - sey,

Chick - en on the fence post, can't dance Jo - sey,

Chick - en on the fence post, can't dance Jo - sey,

Hel - lo, Su - san Brown - y - o.

Read High *Do* and Sixteenth Notes

Jingle at the Window

Singing Game

Pass one win - dow, ti - de - o,   Pass two win - dows, ti - de - o,

Pass three win - dows, ti - de - o,   Jin - gle at the win - dows, ti - de - o.

Ti - de - o,   ti - de - o,   Jin - gle at the win - dows, ti - de - o.

The pitches *do re mi so la* make up a *pentatonic*, or five-tone, scale. Sing the pentatonic scale, ending with high *do*.

SING these patterns with pitch syllables, then find them in the song. Which pattern has high *do*?

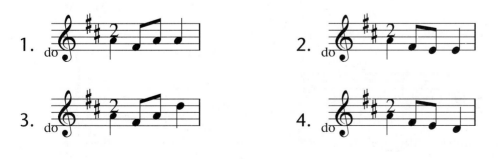

1.

2.

3.

4.

Hop Up, My Ladies

Virginia Folk Song

Verse

C

1. Did you ev-er go to meet-ing, Un-cle Joe, Un-cle Joe?
2. Will your horse____ car-ry dou-ble, Un-cle Joe, Un-cle Joe?

C ... G7

Did you ev-er go to meet-ing, Un-cle Joe?____
Will your horse____ car-ry dou-ble, Un-cle Joe?____

C

Did you ev-er go to meet-ing, Un-cle Joe, Un-cle Joe?
Will your horse____ car-ry dou-ble, Un-cle Joe, Un-cle Joe?

F ... G ... C

Don't mind the weath - er, so the wind don't blow.

Refrain

C

Hop up, my la - dies, three in a row, Hop up, my la - dies,

G ... C

three in a row, Hop up, my la - dies, three in a row,

F ... G7 ... C

Don't mind the weath - er, so the wind don't blow.

3. Is your horse a single-footer, . . .   5. Say, you might take a tumble, . . .
4. Say, don't you want to gallop, . . .

Beat Groupings of Three

Old Paint

American Folk Song
Arranged by Mary Goetze

A F   C7   F

Good - bye, Old Paint, I'm a - leav - in' Chey - enne.

Ride!   Ride!   Gid-dy up!   Gid-dy up!

A F   C7   F

Good - bye, Old Paint, I'm a - leav - in' Chey - enne.

Ride!   Ride!   Gid-dy up!   Gid-dy up!

B F   C7   F

I'm a - leav - in' Chey - enne, And I'm off to Mon - tan'. __

Leav - in' Chey - enne.   Off to Mon - tan',

A F   C7   F

Good - bye, Old Paint, I'm a - leav - in' Chey - enne!

Ride!   Ride!   Gid-dy up!   Gid-dy up!

Au clair de la lune
In the Moonlight

French Folk Song
English Version by MMH

French: Au clair de la lu - ne, Mon a - mi Pier - rot,
Pronunciation: o klɛr də la lü nə mõ na mi pyɛ ro
English: Out here in the moon-light, My good friend Pier - rot,

Prê - te moi ta plu - me, Pour é - crire un mot.
prɛ tə mwa ta plü mə pu re kri rɶ̃ mo
Look now, my poor can - dle Will not ev - en glow.

Ma chan-delle est mor - te, Je n'ai plus de feu;
mã shã dɛ lɛ mɔr tə ʒə ne plü də fö
I must write a let - ter, Help me, I im - plore!

Ou - vre moi ta por - te, Pour l'a-mour de Dieu.
u vrə mwa ta pɔr tə pur la mur də dyö
For the love of hea - ven, Op - en up your door!

CLAP or play this rhythm with the song.

374

Reading Rhythms You Know

DISCOVER rhythm and pitch in this song.

- Find the dotted half notes.
- Find two phrases that begin on an upbeat.
- Identify the pitch syllables.

Ezekiel Saw the Wheel

African American Spiritual

E - ze - kiel ___ saw ___ the wheel,

'way up in the mid - dle of the air.

E - ze - kiel ___ saw ___ the wheel,

'way in the mid - dle of the air.

Finding Upbeats

USE these steps to learn this cowboy song:

• **Move to the long sounds in this song.**

• **Find the phrases that begin with upbeats.**

• **Sing the song with pitch syllables.**

Oklahoma Cowboy Song

1. I'm going to leave _____ old __ Tex - as now, _____
2. They've plowed and fenced _____ my __ cat - tle range, _____
3. I've roped and tied _____ the __ dog - ies small, _____
4. I'm gon-na turn my back _____ on the Tex - as sky, _____
5. Say "A - di - os" _____ to the friends I know, _____

They've got no use _____ for the long-horn cow. _____
And the peo-ple there _____ are __ all so strange. _____
And lis-tened for _____ the coy - o - te's call. _____
We'll ride a - way, _____ old __ Paint and I. _____
I'll hit the trail _____ for __ Mex - i - co. _____

Using What You Know

LEARN a new song by following these steps:
- **Find the phrase that begins on an upbeat.**
- **Read the rhythm and pitches.**
- **Add ostinato patterns that use rhythms you know.**
- **Act the song out!**

Snake Baked a Hoecake

Virginia Folk Song

Snake baked a hoe-cake and set a frog to watch it,

And the frog got a nod-ding and a liz-ard came and stole___ it.

Fetch back my hoe-cake, you long-tailed nan-ny, you,

Fetch back my hoe-cake, you long-tailed nan-ny, you.

Singing Songs in Different Ways

Which measures in this Brazilian song go downward
by step?

SING the song legato, marcato, and staccato.
Which is your favorite way?

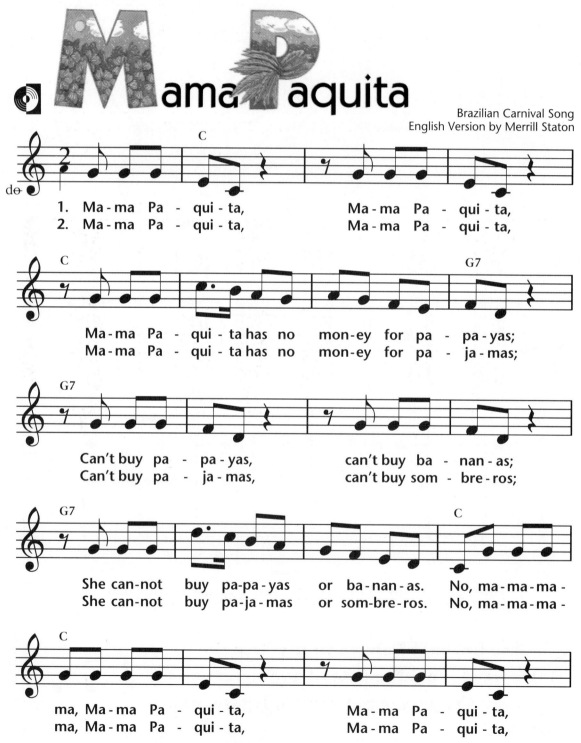

Mama Paquita

Brazilian Carnival Song
English Version by Merrill Staton

1. Ma-ma Pa - qui - ta,   Ma-ma Pa - qui - ta,
2. Ma-ma Pa - qui - ta,   Ma-ma Pa - qui - ta,

Ma-ma Pa - qui - ta has no   mon-ey for pa - pa-yas;
Ma-ma Pa - qui - ta has no   mon-ey for pa - ja-mas;

Can't buy pa - pa-yas,   can't buy ba - nan-as;
Can't buy pa - ja-mas,   can't buy som - bre-ros;

She can-not   buy pa-pa-yas   or ba-nan-as.   No, ma-ma-ma -
She can-not   buy pa-ja-mas   or som-bre-ros.   No, ma-ma-ma -

ma, Ma-ma Pa - qui - ta,   Ma-ma Pa - qui - ta,
ma, Ma-ma Pa - qui - ta,   Ma-ma Pa - qui - ta,

378

Ma - ma Pa - qui - ta will not   have a ripe pa - pa - ya;
Ma - ma Pa - qui - ta will not   have the fine pa - ja - mas;

No ripe pa - pa - ya,   no ripe ba - nan - a,
No fine pa - ja - mas,   no fine som - bre - ros,

So   go   to   Car - ni - val   to   laugh and dance and   sing.

C   D   E   F   G   A   B   C   D

What is the tonal center of "Mama Paquita"?

USE the keyboard above to practice the
downward moving parts of the song. Can
you play the passages marcato, legato, and
staccato?

Tonal Center: *Do* or *La*?

Find the tonal center of this Mexican song.

¡QUÉ LLUEVA! IT'S RAINING!

Mexican Children's Game Song

Spanish: **1.–2.** Que llue - va, que llue - va, la ra - na es - tá en la
Pronunciation: **1.–2.** ke ywe βa ke ywe βa la ɾa nɑes tɑen la
English: **1.–2.** It's rain - ing, it's rain - ing, the frog is in the

cue - va; los pa - ja - ri - tos can - tan, la lu - na se le -
kwe βa los pa xa ɾi tos kan tan la lu na se le
cave, And the par - a - keets are sing - ing, the sil - ver moon is

van - ta. Que sí, que no!
βan ta ke si ke no
ris - ing. Oh, yes! Oh, no!

1. Que cai - ga un cha - pa - rron.
ke kai gaun cha pa ɾon
The rain is fall - ing down.
2. Le can - ta el la - bra - dor.
le kan tael la βɾa ðoɾ
The farm - er sings the song.

380

Putting It All Together

FIND high *do* in this song.

There's a Little Wheel A-Turnin'

African American Folk Song

1. There's a lit-tle wheel __ a-turn-in' in my heart.
2. There's a lit-tle bell __ a-ring-in' in my heart.
3. There's a lit-tle song __ a-sing-in' in my heart.

There's a lit-tle wheel __ a-turn-in' in my heart.
There's a lit-tle bell __ a-ring-in' in my heart.
There's a lit-tle song __ a-sing-in' in my heart.

In my heart, _____ in my heart. _____

There's a lit-tle wheel __ a-turn-in' in my heart.
There's a lit-tle bell __ a-ring-in' in my heart.
There's a lit-tle song __ a-sing-in' in my heart.

You're Invited
VIOLIN RECITAL

What do you see in this picture?

A **recital** is a concert given by a solo musician. A soloist usually performs with some kind of accompaniment, like a piano. The soloist has studied and practiced, and would like to share his or her work with others. Friends, family, and other music lovers may attend the recital.

A longer recital may have an **intermission.** An intermission is a short break between the selections of a concert. At intermission, the audience may stretch their legs, eat snacks, or chat with friends.

LISTEN to a violin recital.

LISTENING

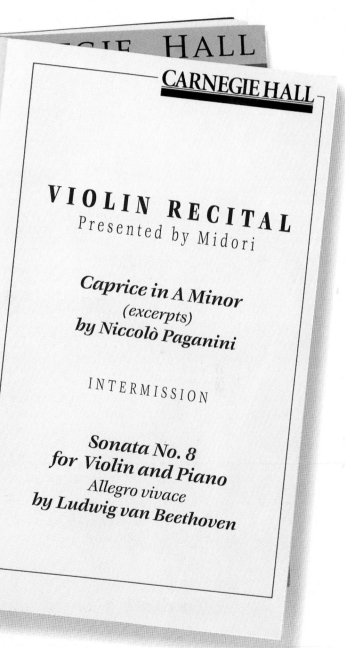

CARNEGIE HALL

V I O L I N R E C I T A L
Presented by Midori

Caprice in A Minor
(excerpts)
by Niccolò Paganini

INTERMISSION

Sonata No. 8
for Violin and Piano
Allegro vivace
by Ludwig van Beethoven

Show your appreciation by clapping. Is this the same way you would show your appreciation at a baseball game? Why?

Listening

Some of the music listed below is very old, and some is new. Which type of music would you like to learn more about?

El grillo
JOSQUIN DES PREZ
1504

Minuet in G
from *Notebook for Anna Magdalena Bach*
CHRISTIAN PETZOLD
1725

Eine Kleine Nachtmusik
First Movement
WOLFGANG AMADEUS MOZART
1787

Discoveries

Clair de lune
from *Suite bergamasque*
CLAUDE DEBUSSY
1905

Cortège
LILI BOULANGER
1914

"Classical" Symphony
Third Movement
SERGEI PROKOFIEV
1917

Inventive Minds

An original musical by Steve and Kathy Hoover

Stuart arrives at school thinking about last night's homework assignment: List the Ten Most Important Inventions in History. Stuart couldn't choose only ten. His list has one hundred twenty-seven! He joins his class to discuss favorite inventions.

Modern Conveniences

Words and Music by
Steve and Kathy Hoover

Verse 1 - solo
Verse 2 - all

1. Mod - ern con - ve - nien - ces are ev' - ry - where.___ In the
2. Fast - er tech - nol - o - gy is what we need.___ A com -

cit - ies and farms___ and towns___ out there.___
put - er that thinks___ with blaz - ing speed!

Mod - ern con - ve - nien - ces are ev' - ry - where,___ and they're
Fast - er tech - nol - o - gy is what we need,___ if we

chang - ing our lives___ each day.___ Yes, they're
want to get by___ to - day,___ if we

1. chang - ing in ev' - ry way!___

2. want to have time___ to play!___

Later on, in the playground, all the children are talking about building inventions for the Invention Fair. Stuart has lots of ideas, but none of them seem just right.

I Need an Idea

Words and Music by
Steve and Kathy Hoover

1. I need an i - de - a,_____ Not just an - y i -
2. I must have a plan,_____ Not just an - y old

de - a._____ It's got - ta be great! It's got - ta be
plan._____ It's got - ta be good. It's got - ta be

1. wow! And I need it right now!_____
   grand!

2. A won - der - ful plan!_____ My teach - er

says_____ to think_____ it through_____ and

388

The children discover more about inventors. Thomas
Edison invented 1,093 things, including electric lights.
Margaret Knight, who invented paper bags, had her first
patent at age 12, and Ruth Wakefield invented chocolate
chip cookies—something almost everyone appreciates!

Thank You

Words and Music by
Steve and Kathy Hoover

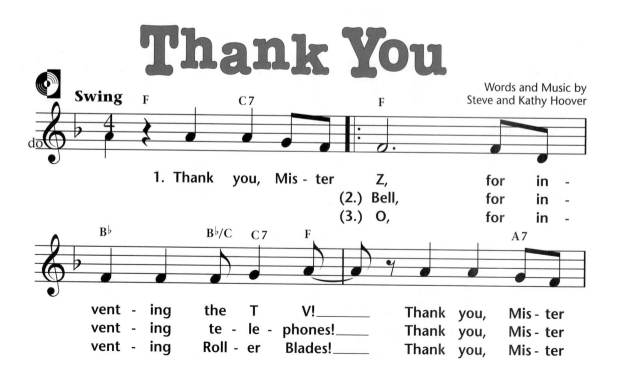

Z,   for all the shows we see!_____ Great
Bell,   for con - nect - ing all our homes!_____ Your
O,   for bright - 'ning all our days!_____ My

Grand - pa loved the ra - di - o, but
best friends may move far a - way, but
Mom says roll - er skates were cool, but

I need a re - mote con - trol! Thank you, Mis - ter
you can call them an - y day. Thank you, Mis - ter
I say it's the blades that rule! Thank you, Mis - ter

Z,   for in - vent - ing the T V!_____
Bell,   for in - vent - ing te - le - phones!__
O,   for in - vent - ing Roll - er Blades!__

1., 2.   F   C7   3. F   2

__   2.,3. Thank you, Mis - ter   __   (whisper) yeah!

An inventor may have to try hundreds of ideas before finding one that works.

Follow Your Dreams

1st time - solo
2nd time - all

Words and Music by
Steve and Kathy Hoover

Fol - low your dreams, though it may seem hard.

Nev - er give up, just reach for the stars.

Fol - low your dreams, though skies may be

gray. Be - lieve in your - self ev - 'ry day.

Stuart has finally decided what to invent!

I've Got an Idea!

Words and Music by
Steve and Kathy Hoover

I've got an i - de - a!_____

It's the great - est i - de - a!_____

I just took my time, and made up my mind.

Now I've got an i - de - a!_____

(spoken) I've got an i - de - a!_____

Finally the day of the Invention Fair is here. Stuart
can't wait to show his invention. He names it "Stuart's
Decision Maker!"

Inventive Minds

Words and Music by
Steve and Kathy Hoover

1st time - solo or small group
2nd time - all

In - ven - tions can change the world, you may say. But did you know we're in - ven - tors to - day? And now just like Or - ville and Wil - bur Wright, Our i - de - as are start- - ing to take flight!

We all have in-ven - tive____ minds._

____ We're think-ing of new____ i - deas____ all the time.__

____ Yes, kids have in-ven - tive____ minds._

____ We're us-ing them ev' - ry day____ of our lives!

(clap)

- ry day____ of our lives!____

(clap)

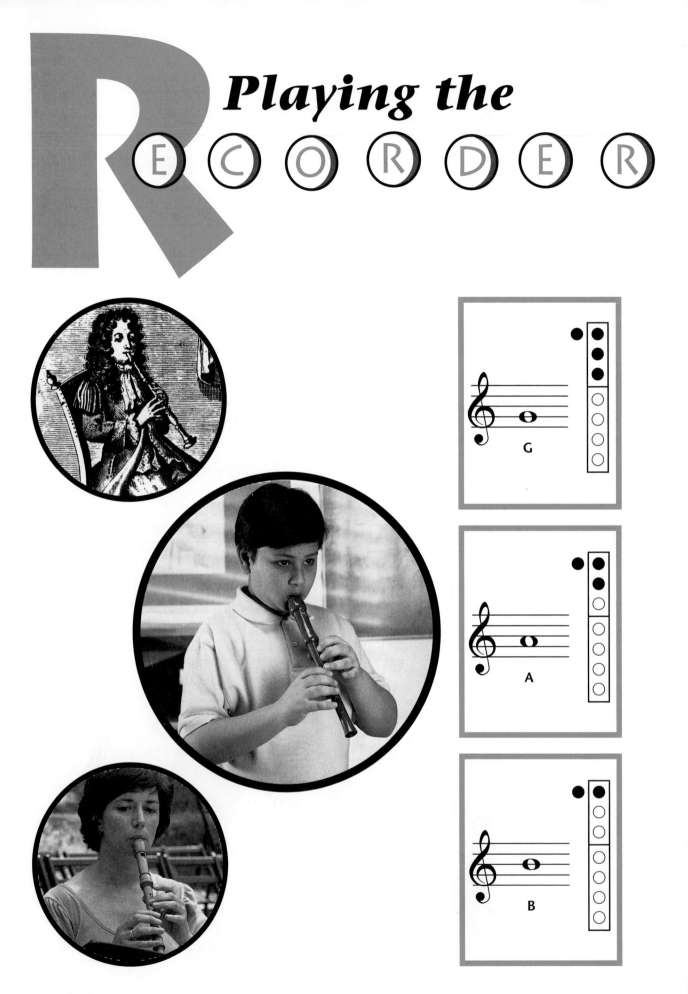

Playing the RECORDER

GLOSSARY

A

accelerando to get faster gradually, **76**

accompaniment a musical background to a melody, **218**

Appalachian dulcimer also known as a zither; a stringed instrument played with both hands: one hand plucks one of the three strings as the other holds or stops the strings near the end, **273**

B

ballet a story told through dance and music, **20**

bar line (|) a line that marks the end of a measure, **30**

C

canon a piece of music in which the melody is introduced and then imitated one or more times; similar to a round, **93, 181**

cello the second-largest instrument in the violin family; it is held between the knees and played by bowing or plucking the strings, **58, 270**

chord three or more pitches sounded together, **221**

coda an ending section to a piece of music, **188**

conduct to lead performers using hands, **124**

crescendo (◁) to get louder gradually, **91**

D

decrescendo (▷) to get softer gradually, **91**

dotted half note (♩.) a note equal to one half note plus one quarter note, **223**

dotted quarter note (♩.) a note equal to one quarter note plus one eighth note, **127**

dotted quarter rest (𝄾·) a rest equal to one quarter rest plus one eighth rest, **128**

double bass or bass the largest instrument in the violin family; it is held upright and played by bowing or plucking the strings, **58, 250**

downbeat the strong beat, **124**

dynamics the loudness or softness of music, **44, 90**

E

eighth note (♪) two eighth notes equal two sounds to a beat (♫), **30**

equal rhythm two sounds of the same length to a beat, **116**

F

fermata (𝄐) a symbol placed over a note to show that it should be held longer than its normal value, **48**

fife and drum an ensemble in which the fife, an instrument from the woodwind family, carries the melody as the drum, from the percussion family, provides the rhythm accompaniment, **136**

first ending (⌐1.⌐) a sign that tells you to go back to the beginning of the song and sing to the second ending, **276**

folk song a song that emerged from the culture of a group of people, usually of unknown authorship, **114**

forte (*f*) loud, **44**

G

guitar a popular member of the stringed instrument family; it has either six or twelve strings and is played by strumming, plucking, or picking, **192, 220–221**

H

half note (♩) a note that shows a sound that is two beats long, **79**

harp one of the oldest stringed instruments; the orchestral harp has a large, triangle-like frame that holds 46 strings and 7 pedals; it stands upright and is played by plucking or strumming the strings, **106–107**

heavier voice quality of singing or speaking that usually gives louder, fuller, and lower sound, **24**

I

intermission a short break between selections of a concert, **383**

introduction music that comes before a song or composition, **188**

L

ledger line an extra line added above or below the staff, **130**

legato smoothly, **261**

lighter voice quality of singing or speaking that gives quieter, generally higher sound, **24**

lute a stringed instrument with a pear-shaped back; it usually has 20 strings and, like the guitar, is played by strumming, plucking, or picking the strings, **232–233, 241**

M

marcato with extra force, **261**

mariachi a Mexican instrumental group that may include trumpets, violins, guitars, a guitarrón, a vihuela, and a small harp, **192–193**

measure a unit used to group notes and rests, **30**

melodic ostinato a short melody that repeats over and over, **141**

melody the tune; a series of pitches moving upward, downward, or staying the same, **18**

meter signature the symbol that tells how many beats are grouped in each measure and what kind of note equals one beat, **30**

O

orchestra a large group of instrumental performers, usually including four families of instruments: strings, woodwinds, brass, and percussion, **58–61**

ostinato a musical pattern that repeats over and over, **139, 164**

P

pentatonic having five pitches, **185**

pentatonic scale a five-tone scale, **185**

phrase a short section of music that is one musical thought, **167**

piano (*p*) soft, **44**

pitch the highness or lowness of a sound, **18, 36**

pitch syllable the name of a pitch, such as do or re, **39**

pizzicato played by plucking a stringed instrument, **250**

Q

quarter note (♩) a musical sign that shows one sound to a beat, **30**

quarter rest (𝄽) a musical sign that shows a beat with no sound, **30**

R

recital a concert given by a solo musician, **382**

recorder a small member of the woodwind family; it has eight finger holes and is played by blowing into a mouthpiece, **232, 241**

refrain a section of a song that is repeated after each verse, **70**

repeat one way a melody moves; staying on the same pitch, **170**

repeat sign (⫶‖) a symbol that tells you to repeat part of a piece of music, **138**

rhythm combinations of longer and shorter sounds and silences, **13, 42**

rhythm pattern an organized group of long and short sounds that repeats, **15**

rondo a piece of music in which the A section always returns; the sections in between are different (A B A C A), **192**

S

scale a group of pitches in order from lowest to highest, **185**

scat a type of singing that began as singers imitated jazz instrument sounds; uses nonsense syllables sung in melodies, **286**

second ending (⌜2.⎯⎯⎯⎯) the ending after the first ending, **276**

sixteenth note (♪) four sixteenth notes equal one beat (♫♫), **174**

skip one way a melody moves; to move higher or lower by jumping over one or more pitches, **170**

slur (⌣) a symbol that tells you to sing a syllable on more than one pitch, **130**

speech piece words set to a rhythm with no melody, **13**

spiritual an African American folk song, many of which began as religious songs, **132**

staccato short and light, **261**

staff the five lines and four spaces on which musical notes are written, **36**

step one way a melody moves; to move higher or lower to the next pitch, **170**

string family instruments such as violin, viola, cello, and double bass that are sounded by plucking or by drawing a bow across strings, **58**

synthesizer an electronic instrument that can create sounds or imitate the tone colors of traditional instruments, **86**

T

tempo the speed of the beat, **74**

tie (‿) a curved line that connects two notes of the same pitch and means that the sound should be held for the length of both notes, **79**

tonal center the home tone or pitch around which a melody seems to center; often the last pitch, **264**

tone color the special sound of each instrument or voice, **24**

treble clef or G clef (𝄞) tells that the notes on the second line of a staff are called G, **236**

U

unequal rhythm two sounds of unequal lengths to a beat, **116**

upbeat the weak beat before the downbeat, **124**

V

verse a section of a song that is repeated using the same melody but different words, **70**

viola a stringed instrument slightly larger than the violin; it is held under the chin and played by bowing or plucking the strings, **58**

violin the smallest instrument in the string family; it is held under the chin and played by bowing or plucking the strings, **61, 204–205, 270**

violoncello see **cello**, **58, 270**

W

whole note (𝅝) a note to show a sound that lasts four beats, **224**

whole rest (▬) a rest to show a silence that lasts four beats, **224**

ACKNOWLEDGMENTS *continued*

Jonico Music, Inc. for *Swing Up High*. Words and music by Joe Raposo.

Lakeview Music Co. Ltd., London, England & TRO-Hollis Music Inc., New York, NY, for *Who Will Buy?* Words and music by Lionel Bart.

Little House Music for *The World Is a Rainbow*. Words and music by Gregory Paul Scelsa.

Memphis Musicraft Publications for *Halloween Night* by Doris Parker and *They're Out of Sight* by Michael D. Bennett from HOLIDAYS–21 FESTIVE ARRANGEMENTS, Copyright © 1980 Michael D. Bennett. Published by Memphis Musicraft Publications, 3149 Southern Ave., Memphis, TN 38111.

MGA for *Rattlesnake Skipping Song* by Dennis Lee, from ALLIGATOR PIE, published by Macmillan of Canada, Copyright © 1974 Dennis Lee.

MMB Music, Inc. for *Oh Lord, I Want Two Wings* from CHATTER WITH THE ANGELS by Shirley McRae. © 1980 MMB Music, Inc., Saint Louis. Used by Permission. All Rights Reserved for *Old Paint* and *The Old Sow's Hide* from THE CAT CAME BACK by Mary Goetze. © 1984 MMB Music, Inc., Saint Louis. Used by Permission. All Rights Reserved.

Music Sales Corporation for *Cortège* from DEUX MORCEAUX POUR VIOLON ET PIANO by Lili Boulanger. Copyright © 1918, 1981 by G. Schirmer, Inc. (ASCAP). International Copyright Secured. All Rights Reserved. Reprinted by Permission.

Music Sales Corp. for *Swinging on a Star*. Words and music by Johnny Burke and James Van Heusen.

Harold Ober Associates, Inc. for *Carol of the Brown King* by Langston Hughes. Reprinted by permission of Harold Ober Associates Incorporated. Copyright © 1958 by Crisis Pub. Co. Copyright renewed 1986 by George Houston Bass.

University of Oklahoma Press for *Señor Don Juan de Pancho* and *Veinte y tres* from HISPANIC FOLK MUSIC OF NEW MEXICO AND THE SOUTHWEST, by John Donald Robb. Copyright © 1980 by the University of Oklahoma Press.

Tom O'Leary for *Treasure Chests* by Tom O'Leary. Copyright © 1981 Tom O'Leary.

Oxford University Press for *Biddy, Biddy (Lost My Gold Ring)* from BROWN GAL IN DE RING by Olive Lewin. Copyright © 1974 Oxford University Press for *Every Night When the Sun Goes In* from FOLK SONGS OF THE SOUTHERN APPALACHIANS by Cecil Sharp. By permission of Oxford University Press.

Peter Pauper Press for *Ashes My Burnt Hut* by Hokushi. Copyright © Peter Pauper Press.

Prentice-Hall, Inc. for *Telephone Song* from THE KODALY CONTEXT, p. 236, by Lois Choksy, copyright © 1981. Reprinted by permission of Prentice-Hall Inc., Englewood Cliffs, NJ.

G.P. Putnam's Sons for *The Hungry Waves* by Dorothy Aldis, reprinted by permission of G.P. Putnam's Sons from HERE, THERE AND EVERYWHERE, copyright 1927, 1928, © 1955, 1956 by Dorothy Aldis.

Random House, Inc. for *Alphabet Stew* by Jack Prelutsky from THE RANDOM HOUSE BOOK OF POETRY FOR CHILDREN, selected and introduced by Jack Prelutsky. Copyright © 1983 by Jack Prelutsky. Reprinted by permission of Random House, Inc.

Recordo Music Publishers for *Rockin' Robin*. Music and words by Jimmie Thomas (Leon René).

Marian Reiner for *Bicycle Riding* by Sandra Liatsos. Copyright © 1984 by Sandra Liatsos. This poem appeared originally in CRICKET. Reprinted by permission of Marian Reiner for the author. For Calendar from A SONG I SANG TO YOU by Myra Cohn Livingston. Copyright © 1984, 1969, 1967, 1965, 1959, 1958 by Myra Cohn Livingston. Reprinted by permission of Marian Reiner for the author.

Regent Music Corporation for *Do You Hear What I Hear?*. Words and music by Noel Regney and Gloria Shayne.

Rockhaven Music for *Mama Paquita*, a carnival song from Brazil. English lyrics by Merrill Staton © 1986 Rockhaven Music. For *Pat-a-pan*, lyrics by Merrill Station © 1987 Rockhaven Music.

Sam Fox Publishing Co., Inc. for *The Happy Wanderer*. Music by Freidrich W. Möller and Antonia Ridge.

G. Schirmer, Inc. for *The Sleigh* by Ivor Tchervanow and Richard Kountz.

Scholastic, Inc. for *¡Qué llueva!* from ARROZ CON LECHE: POPULAR SONGS AND RHYMES FROM LATIN AMERICA, selected by Lulu Delacre. Copyright © 1989 by Lulu Delacre. Reprinted by permission of Scholastic, Inc.

Charles Scribner's Sons for *Carol* from THE WIND IN THE WILLOWS by Kenneth Grahame. Reprinted with permission of Charles Scribner's Sons, an imprint of Macmillan Publishing Company. Copyright 1933, 1953 Charles Scribner's Sons; copyrights renewed © 1961 Ernest H. Shepard and 1981 Charles Scribner's Sons and Mary Eleanor Jessie Knox.

Shada Music Inc. for *I'd Like to Teach the World to Sing* by Bill Backer, Billy Davis, Roger Cook, and Roger Greenaway. © Shada Music Inc. Used By Permission.

Kathy B. Sorensen for *Deta, Deta*; *Oma Rapeti*; *Tititorea*; and *Wang Ü Ger*; collected and transcribed by Kathy B. Sorensen. Copyright © 1991 Kathy B. Sorensen.

Staff Music Publishing Co., Inc. for *One, Two, Three!*, words and music by Maurice Gardner. Written in the style of a Barbados Work Song. Copyright © 1961 Staff Music Publishing Co., Inc.

Sweet Pipes Inc. for *Kuma San* from MELODIES FROM THE FAR EAST by Marilyn Copeland Davidson. Copyright © 1990 Sweet Pipes Inc. Used by permission.

Warner Brothers Publications Inc. for *Autumn to May* by Paul Stookey and Peter Yarrow. © 1962 (Renewed) PEPAMAR MUSIC CORP. All Rights Reserved. Used by Permission. For *Don't Nobody Bring Me No Bad News* by Charlies Smalls. © 1975 WARNER-TAMERLANE PUBLISHING CORP. All Rights Reserved. Used by Permission. For *Rocky Road* by Paul Stookey and Mary Travers. © 1963 (Renewed) PEPAMAR MUSIC CORP. All Rights Reserved. Used by Permission.

Art & Photo Credits

COVER DESIGN: Robert Brook Allen, A Boy and His Dog

COVER PHOTOGRAPHY: All photographs are by the McGraw-Hill School Division except as noted below.

Violin photograph by Artville.

ILLUSTRATION

Steve Adler, 124-125; 132-133; Doug Aitken, 96-97; Steve Armes, 1; Zita Asbaghi, 338-339; George Baquero, 86-87; Rose Mary Berlin, 358; Ami Blackshear, 182-183; Joe Boddy, 312-313; Doug Bowles, 58-59; Alan Brunettin, Thomas Buchs, 316-317, 333; 232-233; Kye Carbone, 20-21; Susan Carlson, 28-29; Ben Carter, 234-235; Tony Chen, 318-319; Brian Cody, 214-215, 242-243; Mary Collier, 112; Connie Conally, 40-41; Floyd Cooper, 16-17, 142-143; Laura Cornell, 72-73, 226-227; Neverne Covington, 192-193; Jerry Dadds, 243; Stephan Daigle, 346-347; Robert Dale 32-33; Lisa Desimini, 278-279; David Diaz, 12-13; Julie Downing, 336-337; Brian Dugan, 42-43, 194-195; Andrea Eberbach, 180-181, 195; Clifford Faust, 212-213; Greg Fitzhugh, 78-79; Brad Gaber, 106-107, 284-285; Barbara Garrison, 334-335; Cameron Gerlach, 70-71; Robert Giuliani, 233, 269, 271; Jack Graham, 174-175; Susan Greenstein, 92-93; Lane Gregory, 226-227; John Steven Gurney, 310-311; Abe Gurvin, 240-241; Pam-ela Harrelson, 190-191; Thomas Hart, 300-301; Kevin Hawkes, 186-187; Mitch Heinze, 64-65; Terry Herman, 208-209, 310, 322-323; Jennifer Hewitson, 164-165, 194; Celina Hinojosa, 282-283; Catherine Huerta, 234-235; Susan Huls, 340-341; Michael Ingle, 380; Chet Jeziersky, 68-69; Victoria Kann, 158-159; Mark Kaplan, 30-31; Deborah Keats, 264-265; Christa Kieffer, 216-217, 243; Mary King, 236-237; Kathleen Kinkoff, 288-289; Terry Kovalcik, 46-47; Sophia Latto, 272-273; Bryce Lee, 120-121; Fran Lee, 34-35, 51; Richard Leonard, 26-27, 206-207, 242; Steve Madson, 22-23; Benton Mahon, 345; Michael McCurdy, 108-109; Larry Mikec, 386-387, 388, 390, 391, 392, 393, 395; Verlin Miller, 80-81; Yoshi Miyake, 154-155; Christian Musselman, 100-101; Tom Nachreiner, 330, 376; Michele Noiset, 162-163, 194, 292-293; Yoshikazu Ogino, 318-319; Ed Parker, 18-19, 50-51; Jerry Pavey, 166-167, 194-195; Bob Pepper, 114-115, 126-127, 135, 145-147; Evangelia Philippidis, 260-261; Jean Pidgeon, 122-123, 205; Bob Radigan, 40-41, 188-189; Victoria Raymond, 230-231; Lynn Rowe Reed, 90-91; Barbara Reid 244-245; Glenn Reid, 76-77; Anna Rich, 142-143; Kumiko Robinson, 268-269, 344; Kristina Rodanas, 178-179; Sergio Roffo, 66-67; Robert Roper, 110-111, 130-131, 146-149; Joanna Roy, 241; Kristi Schaeppi, 330-331; John Schilling, 314-315; Karen Schmidt, 94-95; Bob Scott, 52-53; Marti Shohet, 320-321; Geo Sipp, 74-75; Joe Spencer, 98-99; Mary Spencer, 130-131; Ken Spengler, 168-169, 195, 254-255; Chris Spollen, 184-185; Michael Steirnagle, 38-39; Joyce Stiglich, 10-11; Susan Swan, 128-129; Peggy Tagel, 24-25, 218-219, 348-349; Julia Talcott, 304-305; Angelo Tillery, 8-9; Winson Trang, 84-85, 172-173; John Turano, 342-343; Cornelius van Wright, 328-329; Dale Verzaal, 36-37; Mark Weakley, 62-63; Richard Weber, 138-139, 294-295; Jonathan Wood, 82-83; Susan Hunt Yule, 308-309; Jerry Zimmerman, 44-45.

Tech Art by TCA Graphics, Inc.

PHOTOGRAPHY

All photographs are by the McGraw-Hill School Division (MHSD) except as noted below:

i: r. © Artville. iv. l. © Artville; l. © Artville. v: r. © Artville. vi: l. © Artville; r. © Artville. vii: drumsticks, © Artville; flute, © Artville. **Unit 1** 15: Scott Harvey for MHSD. 17: John Ahearn/Brooke Alexander Gallery NY. 24: Vocal Dynamics Lab/Center for Communications Disorders/Lenox Hill Hospital. 27: Jim Powell Studio for MHSD. 28-29: t. Scott Harvey for MHSD. 30: l. Annie Griffiths Belt/Westlight. 31: l. William Strode/Woodfin Camp & Associates, Inc.; r. Sobel/Klonski/The Image Bank; r. Michal Heron/Woodfin Camp & Associates, Inc. 33: Archiv Fur Kunst Und Geschicte, Berlin/Photo Researchers, Inc. 21: The Collection of E. Van Hoorick/Superstock. 42: t.l. Archiv Fur Kunst Und Geschicte, Berlin/Photo Researchers, Inc. 48: Diane Padys/FPG International. 50, 51: Bill Waltzer for MHSD. 58-59: Mathers Museum. **Unit 2** 62-63: David Jeffrey/The Image Bank. 74: b.r. Jack Vartoogian. 77: t.r. Museum of Modern Art, NY, Gift of Abby Aldrich Rockefeller. 84: Scott Harvey for MHSD. 87-88: FPG International; b. NASA/FPG International. 88: t.r. Kazunobu Yanagi. 88-89: Patrick Eden/The Image Bank. 89: b.r. Giraudon/Art Resource. 94: Scott Harvey for MHSD. 97: Scott Harvey for MHSD. **Unit 3** 116-117: Adstock Photos/Don B. Stevenson. 118-119: bkgnd. M. Angelo/Westlight. 124: John Running. 125: The Granger Collection. 136-137: George Mars Cassidy/Picture Cube; Alon Reininger/Woodfin Camp & Associates, Inc. 21: Scott Harvey for MHSD. 140: l. The Bettmann Archive. 140-141: b. Roy King. 141: r. Guido Alberto Rossi/The Image Bank. 144: Dennis Brack/Black Star; b., m., t. Scott Harvey for MHSD. 146-147: bkgnd. M. Angelo/Westlight. 147: b. Don B. Stevenson/Adstock. 154: M. Angelo/Westlight; b.l. Owen Seumptewa. 155: Eric Haase. 156: t.l. John Running. 156-157: b.r., m., t.l. John Running. 157: b.r. Courtesy Scohoharie Museum of the Iroquois Indian; m. Courtesy University of South Dakota. **Unit 4** 170-171: Steven Studd/Tony Stone Worldwide. 176: Salzburg Museo di Mozart/Scala/Art Resource. 177: Robert Frerck/Woodfin Camp & Associates, Inc. 197: Bill Waltzer for MHSD. 202-203: m.l. Colonial Williamsburg Foundation. 204: © 1993 John Terence Turner/FPG International. 205: l. Scott Harvey for MHSD. 205: Jim Powell Studio for MHSD. **Unit 5** 206-207: Lance Nelson/Stock Market. 186: t. Susan Wilson. 220-221: b. Jim Powell Studio for MHSD. 224-225: Tony Craddock/Tony Stone Worldwide. 228-229: b. Benjamin Randel/Stock Market. 232: Giraudon/Art Resource. 238: Kunstsammlung Nordrhein-Westfalen, Dusseldorf. 239: Courtesy of Andre Emmerich Gallery, New York. 250: Chad Ehlers/Allstock. 251: Courtesy Aca Galleries, NY. The Estate of Romare Bearden. 252-253: Frank Micelotti. **Unit 6** 259: Courtesy U.S. Committee For Unicef/Scott Harvey for MHSD. 261: b. Marc Romanelli/The Image Bank; m. Doug Armand/Tony Stone Worldwide; t. Bill Ross/Westlight. 267: b. Leo Castelli Gallery; t. The Metropolitan Museum of Art, The Jules Bache Collection, 1940. 268: Christian Steiner/courtesy Sony Classical. 270-271: Jim Powell Studio for MHSD. 232: Chun Y Lai/Esto Photographics. 273: George Pickow. 274-275: Brown Brothers. 276-277: Trevle Wood. 240: Art Resource. 286: Ken Regan/Camera 5; b.m. Jim Powell Studio for MHSD. 287: Jim Powell Studio for MHSD. 290-291: Jim Stratford. 300-301: b. Scott Harvey for MHSD; t.m. Teri Bloom. 301: r. Teri Bloom. 302-303: b. Rafael Wollman/Gamma Liaison; t. Jean Marc Giboux/Gamma Liaison. **Celebrations** 306-307: t. Rafael Macia/Photo Researchers, Inc. 308: Ken Karp for MHSD; Courtesy Harold Leventhal Assoc. 317: l. Francene Keery/Stock Boston; r. Trip/A Tovy. 330–331: Ken Karp for MHSD. 342: Walton's Musical Instrument Galleries, Ltd. 350: t. Bob Daemmrich/Photo, Inc.; b. Dave Bartruff/Nawrocki Stock Photo, Inc. 351: Bob Daemmrich/Photo, Inc. **Music Library** 382-383: b. Clint Clemens. 383: l., r. Ken Karp for MHSD. 384: b.l. Violin courtesy Sam Ash Music; Eine Kleine Nachtmusik, Library of Congress; r. Courtesy Dresden/Meissen Antique Import Corp., New York. 385: l. Photo, Roger-Viollet, Paris. 396: t. Corbis/Bettman. m. Ken Karp for MHSD; b. 396: Herb Snitzer.

McGraw-Hill School Division thanks The Selmer Company, Inc., and its Ludwig/Musser Industries and Glaesel String Instrument Company subsidiaries for providing all instruments used in MHSD photographs in this music textbook series, with exceptions as follows: MHSD thanks Yamaha Corporation of America for French horn, euphonium, acoustic and electric guitars, soprano, alto, and bass recorders, piano, and vibraphone; MMB Music Inc., St. Louis, MO, for Studio 49 instruments; Rhythm Band Instruments, Fort Worth, TX, for resonator bells; Courtly Instruments, NY, for soprano and tenor recorder; Elderly Instruments, Lansing, MI, for autoharp, dulcimer, hammered dulcimer, mandolin, Celtic harp, whistles, and Andean flute.

CLASSIFIED INDEX

FOLK

African
Ema, Ma, **346**
Jambo (Hello), **12**
Ɔboɔ Asi Me Nsa, **16**

African American
Amen, **329**
Chatter with the Angels, **357**
Children, Go Where I Send Thee, **325**
Don't Nobody Bring Me No Bad News, **262**
Down by the River, **26**
Draw a Bucket of Water, **120**
Ezekiel Saw the Wheel, **375**
Goin' to Ride Up in the Chariot, **171**
Good News, **260**
Good-bye My Riley O, **297**
I Got a Letter, **284**
I'm on My Way to Freedom Land (Adaptation of
   a traditional song) (listening), **339**
Michael, Row the Boat Ashore, **6**
Miss Mary Mack, **56**
My Good Old Man, **311**
Now Let Me Fly, **132**
Oh Lord, I Want Two Wings, **109**
Old Man Moses, **265**
Rise Up, Shepherd, and Follow, **326**
Telephone Song, **356**
There's a Little Wheel A-Turnin', **381**
Wasn't That a Mighty Day?, **324**
Who Built the Ark?, **361**
Woke Up This Morning, **338**
Zudio, **275**

Akan see also African
Ɔboɔ Asi Me Nsa, **16**

American see also African American; Creole; Native
American; Traditional American
Andrew and His Cutty Gun (Traditional fife-and-
   drum music) (listening), **136**
Bonefish, Bluebird (speech piece), **13**
Built My Lady a Fine Brick House, **102**
Chicken on the Fence Post, **370**
Closet Key, **359**
Cotton-Eyed Joe, **352**
Every Night, **224**
Fox, The, **200**
Frog Went A-Courtin', **162**
Golden Ring Around the Susan Girl, **152**
Great Big House, **364**
Home on the Range, **3**
Hop Up, My Ladies, **372**
I'll Rise When the Rooster Crows, **164**
Jickety Can (speech piece), **76**
Jingle at the Window, **371**
Jubilee, **83**
Killy Kranky, **272**
Long-Legged Sailor, **23**

Mabel, Mabel (speech piece), **230**
Old Brass Wagon, The, **199**
Old Paint, **373**
Old Sow's Hide, The, **166**
Old Texas, **376**
One, Two, Three O'Leary, **368**
Piglet's Christmas, The, **335**
Pop! Goes the Weasel, **61**
Rocky Mountain, **18**
Row, Row, Row Your Boat (listening), **129**
Sandy Land, **237**
Sentry Box (Traditional fife-and-drum music)
   (listening), **136**
'Simmons, **365**
Snake Baked a Hoecake, **377**
Sweet Betsy from Pike, **246**
Telephone Song, **356**
There's a Hole in the Bucket, **214**
Turn the Glasses Over, **69**
Vagabond Game (speech piece), **71**

American Indian see Native American

Australian
Kookaburra, **198**

Austrian
Alpine Song, **2**

Bantu see also African
Ema, Ma, **346**

Barbadian see also West Indian
One, Two, Three!, **212**

Brazilian see also Hispanic
Mama Paquita, **378**

Chinese
Wang Ü Ger (Chinese Fishing Song), **172**

Creole
Sweep, Sweep Away, **225**

Czech
Doudlebska Polka (Traditional Czech Polka)
   (listening), **350**

English
Charlie, **127**
Doubtful Shepherd (English Dance Tune)
   (listening), **202**
Here We Come A-Wassailing, **336**
Hot Cross Buns, **359**
Scotland's Burning, **368**

French see also Creole
Au clair de la lune (In The Moonlight), **374**
Frère Jacques (Are You Sleeping?), **151**
Pat-a-Pan, **334**
Ton moulin (Your Windmill), **228**

Hebrew, Israeli, Jewish
Hag Asif (Harvest Time), **316**
Hag Shavuot (Festival of First Fruits), **344**
O Hanukkah, **320**

Hispanic
Acitrón, **353**
Bate, bate (speech piece), **115**
Cuequita de los Coyas (Andean Highlands Folk
    Music) (listening), **213**
El barquito (The Little Boat), **104**
El charro (The Cowboy), **247**
El pájaro campana (The Bell Bird) (Traditional Harp
    Music arr. by A. R. Ortiz) (listening), **108**
El tren (The Train), **78**
Juan Pirulero, **366**
Los mariachis (Mexican Folk Music) (listening), **193**
Matarile, **363**
¡Qué llueva! (It's Raining!), **380**
Señor Don Juan de Pancho, **278**
Veinte y tres (Twenty Three), **126**

Irish
Wee Falorie Man, The, **343**

Italian
Farfallina (Butterfly), **362**

Jamaican *see also* West Indian
Biddy, Biddy, **189**
Jamaican Jump-Up by H. C. Mon Solomon
    (listening), **350**

Japanese
Chichipapa (The Sparrows' Singing School), **367**
Deta, Deta (The Moon), **85**
Kuma San (Honorable Bear), **34**
Sakura (Cherry Blossoms), **345**
Yuki (Snow), **318**

Maori
Oma Rapeti (Run, Rabbit), **54**
Tititorea (Maori Stick Game), **210**

Mexican *see also* Hispanic
Bate, bate (speech piece), **137**
El charro (The Cowboy), **247**
Los mariachis (listening), **193**
Matarile, **363**
¡Qué llueva! (It's Raining!), **380**

Native American
Hopi
Hopi Lullaby (listening), **154**
Lakota
Lakota Honor Song (listening), **155**
Luiseño
Kasilyio (The Wet Sage), **198**
Pueblo
Pueblo Corn Grinding Song (listening) **154**
Seneca
Seneca Stomp Dance (listening), **235**

Panamanian *see also* Hispanic
El barquito (The Little Boat), **104**

Scottish
Aiken Drum, **103**
Scotland's Burning, **368**

Traditional American
Grandma's Feather Bed, **354**

I'd Like to Teach the World to Sing, **viii**
In the Good Old Summertime (song and
    listening), **351**
Joy to the World, **330**
Row, Row, Row, Your Boat (listening), **129**
This Land Is Your Land, **308**

Venezuelan *see also* Hispanic
El tren (The Train) **78**

Welsh
Deck the Hall, **331**

West Indian
Biddy, Biddy (Jamaica), **189**
Dumplin's, **40**
One, Two, Three! (Barbados), **212**

HOLIDAYS, SEASONAL, PATRIOTIC

Autumn
Autumn to May, **72**
Gather 'Round, **314**

Christmas
Amen, **329**
Children, Go Where I Send Thee, **325**
Deck the Hall, **331**
Do You Hear What I Hear?, **332**
Great Day in December by C. Jeter (listening), **327**
Joy to the World, **330**
Pat-a-Pan, **334**
Piglets' Christmas, The **335**
Rise Up, Shepherd, and Follow, **326**
Sleigh, The, **319**
Wasn't That a Mighty Day? **324**

Earth Day
All Living Things, **348**
Ema, Ma, **346**
From Morning Night to Real Morning (collected
    by S. Feld) (listening), **347**

Halloween
Halloween Night, **312**
My Good Old Man, **311**
They're Out of Sight, **310**

Hanukkah
Eight Days of Hanukkah, The, **322**
O Hanukkah, **320**

Harvest *see also* Sukkot, Shavuot
Gather 'Round, **314**
Hag Asif (Harvest Time), **316**
Hag Shavuot (Festival of First Fruits), **344**
Pueblo Corn Grinding Song (listening), **154**
Thanksgiving Day Is Here (poem), **315**

Martin Luther King, Jr., Day
Goin' to Ride Up in the Chariot, **190**
Good News, **281**
I'm on My Way to Freedom Land (Adaptation of
    a traditional song) (listening), **339**
Now Let Me Fly, **132**
Woke Up This Morning, **338**

New Year's Day
Here We Come A-Wassailing, **336**

Patriotic
America, **309**
America, the Beautiful, **306**
Andrew and His Cutty Gun (Traditional fife- and-drum music) (listening), **136**
Sentry Box (Traditional fife-and-drum music) (listening), **136**
This Land Is Your Land, **308**
Yankee Doodle Boy, **307**
You're a Grand Old Flag, **7**

Shavuot
Hag Shavuot (Festival of First Fruits), **344**

Spring *see also* St. Patrick's Day, Earth Day, Shavuot
Sakura (Cherry Blossoms), **345**

St. Patrick's Day
St. Patrick's Day by L. Rowsome (listening), **342**
Wee Falorie Man, The, **343**

Sukkot
Hag Asif (Harvest Time), **316**

Summer
Acitrón, **353**
Cotton-Eyed Joe, **352**
Doudlebska Polka (Traditional Czech polka) (listening), **350**
In the Good Old Summertime, **351**
In the Good Old Summertime by G. Evans, words by R. Shields (listening), **351**
Jamaican Jump-Up by H.C. Mon Solomon (listening), **350**

Valentine's Day
Frog Went A-Courtin', **162**
Never Gonna Be Your Valentine, **340**
There's a Little Wheel A-Turnin', **381**

Winter *see also* Christmas, Hanukkah, New Year
Sleigh, The, **319**
Yuki (Snow), **318**

MUSICAL

Inventive Minds
Follow Your Dreams, **392**
I Need an Idea, **388**
Inventive Minds, **394**
I've Got an Idea!, **393**
Modern Conveniences, **387**
Thank You, **390**

NON-ENGLISH MUSIC

Akan
Ɔboɔ Asi Me Nsa, **16**

Bantu
Ema, Ma, **346**

Chinese
Wang Ü Ger (Chinese fishing Song), **182**

French
Au clair de la lune (In The Moonlight), **374**
Frère Jacques (Are You sleeping?), **151**
Ton moulin (Your Windmill), **228**

Hebrew
Hag Asif (Harvest Time), **316**
Hag Shavuot (Festival of First Fruits), **344**

Hopi
Hopi Lullaby (listening), **154**

Italian
Farfallina (Butterfly), **362**

Japanese
Chichipapa (The Sparrows' Singing School), **367**
Deta, Deta (The Moon), **85**
Kuma San (Honorable Bear), **34**
Sakura (Cherry Blossoms), **345**
Yuki (Snow), **318**

Lakota
Lakota Honor Song (listening), **155**

Luiseño
Kasilyio (The Wet Sage), **198**

Maori
Oma Rapeti (Run, Rabbit), **54**
Tititorea (Maori Stick Game), **210**

Pueblo
Pueblo Corn Grinding Song (listening), **154**

Spanish
Acitrón, **353**
Bate, bate (speech piece), **115**
El barquito (The Little boat), **104**
El charro (The Cowboy), **247**
El tren (The Train), **78**
Juan Pirulero, **366**
Matarile, **363**
¡Qué llueva! (It's Raining!), **380**
Señor Don Juan de Pancho, **278**
Veinte y tres (Twenty Three), **126**

Swahili
Jambo (Hello), **12**

Yiddish
O Hanukkah, **320**

INDEX OF POETRY

Alphabet Stew by Jack Prelutsky, **158**

Ashes my burnt hut (Haiku) by Hokushi, **345**

Bicycle Riding by Sandra Liatsos, **62**

Calendar by Myra Cohn Livingston, **305**

Carol (excerpt) by Kenneth Grahame, **337**

Carol of the Brown King by Langston Hughes, **328**

Clink! an iced branch falls (Haiku) by Kazue
Mizumura, **88**

Dance of the Animals (Pygmy), **347**

Hungry Waves, The, by Dorothy Aldis, **49**

I Bought a Dozen New-Laid Eggs by
Mother Goose, **365**

Jickety Can (speech piece), Anonymous, **76**

Mabel, Mabel by Carl Withers, **230**

Music by Eleanor Farjeon, **291**

Our Washing Machine by Patricia Hubbell, **365**

Postman, The, Anonymous, **255**

Rattlesnake Skipping Song by Dennis Lee, **124**

Rope Rhyme by Eloise Greenfield, **9**

Secret Song, The, by Margaret Wise Brown, **186**

Thanksgiving Day Is Here by Constance Andrea
Keremes, **315**

They Were My People by Grace Nichols, **207**

World Is Day-Breaking, The, by Sekiya Miyoshi, **111**

INDEX OF LISTENING SELECTIONS

Allemande Tripla from *Suite No. 3 in A*, by
J. H. Schein, **232**

Andrew and His Cutty Gun (Traditional fife- and-
drum music), **136**

Caprice in A minor (excerpts) by N. Paganini, **268**

Clair de lune from *Suite bergamasque* by
C. Debussy, **385**

"Classical" Symphony, Third Movement, by
S. Prokofiev, **385**

Cortège by L. Boulanger, **385**

Cuequita de los Coyas (Andean Highlands Folk
Music), **213**

Different Trains (excerpt) by S. Reich, **75**

Doubtful Shepherd (English Dance Tune), **202**

Doudlebska Polka (Traditional Czechoslovakian
Polka), **350**

Eine Kleine Nachtmusik, First Movement, by
W. A. Mozart, **384**

El grillo by Josquin des Prez, **384**

El pájaro campana (The Bell Bird) arranged by
A. R. Ortiz, **108**

From Morning Night to Real Morning collected by
S. Feld, **347**

Gigue from *Sonata for Violin and Continuo* by
A. Corelli, **125**

Great Day in December by C. Jeter, **327**

Hopi Lullaby, **154**

I'm on My Way to Freedom Land (Adaptation of a
traditional song), **339**

In the Good Old Summertime by G. Evans, words by
R. Shields, **351**

It Don't Mean a Thing If It Ain't Got That Swing by
D. Ellington and I. Mills, **287**

Jamaican Jump-Up by H. C. Mon Solomon, **350**

Lakota Honor Song, **155**

Los mariachis (Mexican Folk Music), **193**

March of the Wooden Soldiers from *Album for the
Young* by P. Tchaikovsky, **264**

Minuet in G from *Notebook for Anna Magdalena Bach*
by C. Petzold, **384**

Montage of Orchestral Sounds, **60**

Night Watch by A. Holborne, **93**

Overture to *The Marriage of Figaro* by W. A. Mozart, **176**

Pueblo Corn Grinding Song, **154**

Row, Row, Row Your Boat (Traditional Round), **129**

Sabre Dance from *Gayane* by A. Khachaturian, **20**

Seneca Stomp Dance by A. Jimerson, **235**

Sentry Box (Traditional fife-and-drum music), **136**

Silver Moon by Kitaro, **86**

Sonata No. 8 for Piano and Violin by
L. van Beethoven, **383**

St. Patrick's Day by L. Rowsome, **342**

"Surprise" Symphony No. 94 (Second Movement)
by F. J. Haydn, **32**

Three Little Words from *Trio Jeepy* by B. Marsalis, **253**

Three Rides at the Park by L. Williams, **140**

Variations on a Theme (excerpts) by A. Lloyd
Webber, **270**

Variations on the Theme "Pop! Goes the Weasel"
(excerpt) by L. Caillet, **61**

Waltz Finale from *The Nutcracker* by
P. Tchaikovsky, **205**

INTERVIEWS

Hinton, Milt, **252**

Midori, **268**

Ortiz, Alfredo Rolando, **108**

Reich, Steve, **74**

Ritchie, Jean, **273**

Rogers, Sally, **220**

INDEX OF SONGS AND SPEECH PIECES

Acitrón, **353**

After School, **57**

Aiken Drum, **103**

All Living Things, **348**

Alpine Song, **2**

Amen, **329**

America, **309**

America, the Beautiful, **306**

Au clair de la lune (In the Moonlight), **374**

Autumn to May, **72**

Bate, bate (speech piece), **115, 137**

Biddy, Biddy, **165, 189**

Bonefish, Bluebird (speech piece), **13**

Built My Lady a Fine Brick House, **102**

Charlie, **114, 128**

Chatter with the Angels, **357**

Chichipapa (The Sparrows' Singing School), **367**

Chicken on the Fence Post, **370**

Children, Go Where I Send Thee, **325**

Closet Key, **359**

Coral, **364**

Cotton-Eyed Joe, **352**

Deck the Hall, **331**

Delta Queen, The, **208**

Deta, Deta (The Moon), **85**

Do You Hear What I Hear?, **332**

Don't Nobody Bring Me No Bad News, **262**

Down by the River, **26, 38**

Draw a Bucket of Water, **120, 131**

Dumplin's, **40**

Eight Days of Hanukkah, The, **322**

El barquito (The Little Boat), **104**

El charro (The Cowboy), **247**

El tren (The Train), **78**

Ema, Ma, **346**

Every Night, **224**

Ezekiel Saw the Wheel, **375**

Farfallina (Butterfly), **362**

Follow Your Dreams, **392**

Fox, The, **200**

Frère Jacques (Are You Sleeping?), **151**

Frog Went A-Courtin', **162**

Gather 'Round, **314**

Goin' to Ride Up in the Chariot, **171, 190**

Golden Ring Around the Susan Girl, **152**

Good News, **260, 281**

Good-bye My Riley O, **297**

Grandma's Feather Bed, **354**

Great Big House, **364**

Hag Asif (Harvest Time), **316**

Hag Shavuot (Festival of First Fruits), **344**

Halloween Night, **312**

Happy Wanderer, The, **65**

Haul Away, Joe, **102**

Here We Come A-Wassailing, **336**

Home on the Range, **3**

Hop Up, My Ladies, **372**

Hot Cross Buns, **359**

I Got a Letter, **258, 284**

I Need an Idea, **388**

I'd Like to Teach the World to Sing, **viii**

I'll Rise When the Rooster Crows, **164, 179**

In the Good Old Summertime, **351**

Inventive Minds, **394**

I've Got an Idea!, **393**

Jambo (Hello), **12**

Jickety Can (speech piece), **76, 91**

Jingle at the Window, **371**

Joy to the World, **330**

Juan Pirulero, **366**

Jubilee, **66**

Kasilyio (The Wet Sage), **198**

Killy Kranky, **272**

Kindergarten Wall, The, **298**

Kookaburra, **198**

Kuma San (Honorable Bear), **34**

Long-Legged Sailor, **23**

Mabel, Mabel (speech piece), **230**

Mama Paquita, **378**

Matarile, **363**

Michael, Row the Boat Ashore, **6**

Miss Mary Mack, **56**

Modern Conveniences, **387**

My Good Old Man, **311**

Never Gonna Be Your Valentine, **340**

Now Let Me Fly, **132**

O Hanukkah, **320**

Ɔbɔɔ Asi Me Nsa, **16**

Oh Lord, I Want Two Wings, **109**

Old Brass Wagon, The, **199**

Old Man Moses, **265**

Old Paint, **373**

Old Sow's Hide, The, **166**

Old Texas, **376**

Oma Rapeti (Run, Rabbit), **54**

One, Two, Three!, **212**

One, Two, Three O'Leary, **368**

Pat-a-Pan, **334**

Piglets' Christmas, The, **335**

Pop! Goes the Weasel, **61**

¡Qué llueva! (It's Raining!), **380**

Rattlesnake Skipping Song (speech piece), **124**

Rise Up, Shepherd, and Follow, **326**

Rockin' Robin, **4**

Rocky Mountain, **18, 37**

Rocky Road, **118, 138**

Row, Row, Row Your Boat, **129**

Sakura (Cherry Blossoms), **345**

Salamanca Market, **177, 180**

Sandy Land, **219, 237**

Scotland's Burning, **368**

Señor Don Juan de Pancho, **278**

'Simmons, **365**

Sleigh, The, **319**

Snake Baked a Hoecake, **377**

Sweep, Sweep Away, **217, 225**

Sweet Betsy from Pike, **246**

Swing Up High, **10**

Swinging on a Star, **160**

Telephone Song, **356**

Thank You, **390**

There's a Hole in the Bucket, **214**, **227**

There's a Little Wheel A-Turnin', **381**

They're Out of Sight, **310**

This Land Is Your Land, **308**

Tititorea (Maori Stick Game), **222**

Ton moulin (Your Windmill), **228**

Treasure Chests, **150**

Turn the Glasses Over, **69**, **80**

Vagabond Game (speech piece), **71**

Veinte y tres (Twenty Three), **126**

Waltzing Matilda, **296**

Wang Ü Ger (Chinese Fishing Song), **172**, **182**

Wasn't That a Mighty Day?, **324**

Wee Falorie Man, The, **343**

Wells Fargo Wagon, The, **256**

We're Off to See the Wizard, **168**

Who Built the Ark?, **361**

Who Will Buy?, **112**

Woke Up This Morning, **338**

World Is a Rainbow, The, **248**

Yankee Doodle Boy, **307**

You're a Grand Old Flag, **7**

Yuki (Snow), **318**

Zudio, **275**

PRONUNCIATION KEY
Simplified International Phonetic Alphabet

VOWELS

a	father	æ	cat
e	ape	ɛ	pet
i	bee	ɪ	it
o	obey	ɔ	paw
u	moon	ʊ	put
ʌ	up	ə	ago

SPECIAL SOUNDS

β	say *b* without touching lips together; *Spanish* nueve, haba
ç	hue; *German* ich
ð	the, *Spanish* todo
n̩	sound n as individual syllable
ö	form [o] with lips and say [e]; *French* adieu, *German* schön
œ	form [ɔ] with lips and say [ɛ]; *French* coeur, *German* plötzlich
ɾ	flipped r; butter
r̄	rolled r; *Spanish* perro
ɫ	click tongue on the ridge behind teeth; *Zulu* ngcwele
ü	form [u] with lips and say [i]; *French* tu, *German* grün
ü	form [ʊ] with lips and say [ɪ]
x	blow strong current of air with back of tongue up; *German* Bach, *Hebrew* Hanukkah, *Spanish* bajo
ʒ	pleasure
ʼ	glottal stop, as in the exclamation "uh oh!" [ˈʌ ˈo]
~	nasalized vowel, such as French bon [bõ]
˥	end consonants *k*, *p*, and *t* without puff of air, such as sky (no puff of air after *k*), as opposed to *kite* (puff of air after *k*)

OTHER CONSONANTS PRONOUNCED SIMILAR TO ENGLISH

ch	cheese	ny	onion, *Spanish* niño
g	go	sh	shine
ng	sing	ts	boats

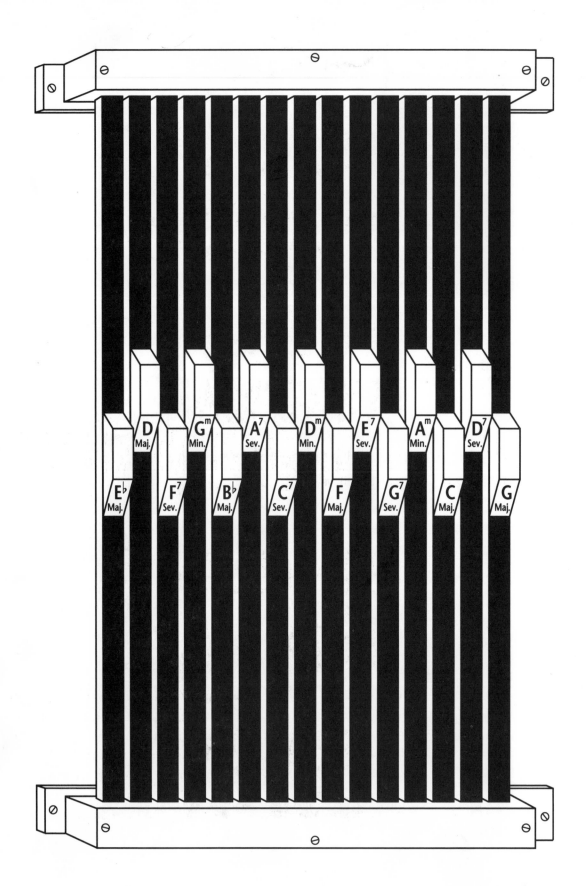